Twilight

Texts and Translations

The Texts and Translations series was founded in 1991 to provide students and teachers with important texts not readily available or not available at an affordable price and in high-quality translations. The books in the series are intended for students in upper-level undergraduate and graduate courses in national literatures in languages other than English, comparative literature, ethnic studies, area studies, translation studies, women's studies, and gender studies. The Texts and Translations series is overseen by an editorial board composed of specialists in several national literatures and in translation studies.

For a complete listing of titles, see the last pages of this book.

ELSA BERNSTEIN

Twilight
A Drama in Five Acts

Translated by
Susanne Kord

The Modern Language Association of America
New York   2003

For information about obtaining permission to reprint material from
MLA book publications or to request the right to perform this work,
send your request by mail (see address below), e-mail (permissions@
mla.org), or fax (646 458-0030).

Library of Congress Cataloging-in-Publication Data

Rosmer, Ernst, 1866–
     [Dämmerung. English]
     Twilight : drama in five acts / Ernst Rosmer (Elsa Bernstein) ;
translated by Susanne Kord.
          p.   cm. — (Texts and translations ; 14)
     Includes bibliographical references.
     ISBN 0-87352-928-6 (pbk.)
     I. Kord, Susanne. II. Title. III. Series.
PT2603.E72 D+   2003
832' .8—dc22   2003044217

     ISSN 1079-2538

Cover illustration: *The Sick Child*, by Edvard Munch, 1885–86. 120 ×
118.5 cm. © 2003 The Munch Museum / The Munch-Ellingsen
Group / Artists Rights Society, New York. National Gallery, Norway.
Photo: J. Lathion.

Printed on recycled paper

Published by The Modern Language Association of America
26 Broadway, New York, New York 10004-1789
www.mla.org

In memoriam
Stephan Pritz (1957–2002)

TABLE OF CONTENTS

ACKNOWLEDGMENTS

My thanks to all who supported this project: Barbara Siegmann (in Würzburg) and Michael Hauptmann (in Hamburg), the author's grandchildren, kindly gave permission for me to reprint and translate the play; Ray Munro, program director of theater arts at Clark University, was immediately interested in having the play performed in my translation; Ray Munro and Virginia Munro collaborated to create the stage version; Virginia Munro found the painting for the cover; Jay Lustbader, director of cornea and refractive surgery, and Teresa Magone, chief resident of ophthamology, both at Georgetown University, confirmed the correctness of clinical and medical terms in English and offered their expertise to clear up some medical mysteries in the play; Markus Rauschecker was the first to read my translation and test the dialogue for colloquial correctness; Lanlan Xu created the transcription of the original.

I also thank all friends in the Kneipe Fetzenreich in Trier (which is the only *Kneipe* in Germany, as far as I'm concerned), where I translated the drama during the summer of 2002: Benedikt Welter corrected a misreading that would have come back to haunt me; Sylvia Krämer made useful suggestions and was stubborn in all the right places; Benedikt Zimmermann ("Want another?"), Ingrid, Kirsi, and Jürgen ("Come on, time for table football!") always knew when I had had it and interrupted at the right time; Sylvia, Benne Zimmermann, and Uta Keller allowed me to continue working ("Just another half page till the end of the scene!!") even after closing time and after all the other customers had been invited to leave in Sylvia's inimitable (and untranslatable) turn of the phrase.

Washington, March 2003

INTRODUCTION

Elsa Bernstein: Her Life, Work, and Reception

Elsa Bernstein can be seen as truly representative of her era, since she participated in most major literary movements of her time. She wrote naturalistic dramas (*Three of Us*, 1891; *Twilight*, 1893; *Maria Arndt*, 1908), impressionist novellas ("Caprice," 1893), neoromantic fairy tales (*Kingly Children*, 1894), a symbolist dramatic requiem (*Mother Mary*, 1900), and neoclassic tragedies (*Nausikaa*, 1906; *Achilles*, 1910). Aside from twenty dramas, of which eight were performed and twelve were printed, she authored numerous novellas and poems. Her last published work is *Das Leben als Drama* (Life as a Drama), memoirs of her incarceration in the concentration camp Theresienstadt between 1942 and 1945, written for her family immediately after her liberation and first published in 1999.

Elsa Porges was born in Vienna in 1866, to Jewish parents. Her father, Heinrich Porges, supposedly an illegitimate son of Franz Liszt, had come to Vienna to further his career as a musician and composer. In 1867, the family moved to Munich, where Porges became a conductor at the court of Ludwig II at Richard Wagner's request. Elsa received an education that left her dissatisfied, but she demonstrated her literary talent early by beginning to write at age seven and publish at age ten (her first drama). After a short but successful career as an actress (1883–87), which she had to give up because of failing eyesight, she returned to writing. Her immediate success as a playwright permitted her to run a literary salon of great renown. She married the Munich lawyer and writer Max Bernstein (1854–1925) in 1890 and had three children with him: Eva (1894–1986, later Eva Hauptmann), Maria (1897; died the same year), and Hans-Heinrich (1898–1980, later Bernt-Atkinson). In 1891, she adopted a male pseudonym, Ernst Rosmer, the name under which she became famous; the only play she wrote that did not appear under this name was *Johannes Herkner* (1904), which she published as Elsa Porges. The bulk of her work was published between 1890 and 1910. Her last published drama, *Fate*, appeared in 1919, followed only by two novellas. Until the Nazis forced her to move in 1939, she ran the literary salon with her sister Gabriele Porges (1868–1942). Thanks to Winifred Wagner's intercession, Bernstein received permission to emigrate to the United States, but she chose to stay in Germany since this permission did not include her sister. Both were deported to Theresienstadt in 1942, where Gabriele died after a few weeks. Bernstein herself survived the experience and went to live with her daughter Eva in Hamburg, where she died in 1949.

Bernstein's dramas are noteworthy for her thorough and unconventional characterization, especially of female figures; her uninhibited language and treatment of taboo subjects (in *Maria Arndt*, certainly the only play of the time to show such a scene, pubescent Gemma is fully informed of the sexual act and the facts of procreation by her mother); and her great attention to realistic detail (for her Greek tragedy *Themistokles* [1896], she did extensive research, learned ancient Greek, and traveled to Greece to visit the sites she described in the drama). A frequent subject of her plays is the culturally sanctioned oppression of women; her female figures are often torn between adherence to social norms and desires for personal autonomy. Bernstein's insistence on a realistic portrayal of her contemporary society is partly expressed in the fact that most of her autonomous heroines are forced back into conventional roles or uphold them voluntarily. The ambivalence and compromising nature of her dramatic endings has disappointed traditional and feminist critics alike. Her greatest success was *Kingly Children*, largely due to the incidental music written for the play by Engelbert Humperdinck, who also rewrote the play as an opera. Bernstein experimented with many forms; her use of style defies analysis in terms of chronological or linear development: she worked simultaneously on her naturalistic drama *Three of Us* and on her neoromantic fairy tale *Kingly Children*; her play *Maria Arndt*, a return to the naturalistic style long after the movement had ended, falls between her neoclassic tragedies *Nausikaa* and *Achilles*.

Her early reception was largely influenced by her choice of genre—as a playwright, she wrote in a genre that at the time was considered the most masculine—and by her readiness to discuss taboo subjects on the stage, occasionally in highly controversial or unconventional terms. Early reviews of her drama *Twilight* were unanimously enthusiastic; famous critics like Alfred Kerr and

Paul Schlenther celebrated her as a new and innovative voice in contemporary drama. Already at the turn of the century, however, her reception began to wane: Adolf Bartels granted her a short and laudatory paragraph (1904); Rudolph Lothar, writing in 1905, subjected her to a highly gendered critique. In a later literary history (1916; Soergel), she is upbraided for the "tastelessness" of her themes (359) but still discussed with some interest; in the nineteenth edition of the same work (1928), she is dismissed as common and unexciting ("All eras have seen phenomena like Ernst Rosmer, and never have they been more frequent than in our day" [405]; all English translations from the German in this introduction are mine). In a revised edition of the same work (1961), the chapter on Bernstein is cut entirely and replaced with a mere paragraph:

> The playwright Max Bernstein lived in Munich; his wife Elsa Porges wrote using the pseudonym Ernst Rosmer. It is astonishing to think that a woman could write such drastic plays. . . . Alfred Kerr was highly enthusiastic about Ernst Rosmer—but he was wrong.   (Soergel and Hohoff 223)

With other literary critics, a similar progression occurs: Robert Arnold, for example, considered Elsa Bernstein "one of the few outstanding female playwrights of German, even world literature" as late as 1912 (304). In a 1925 edition of his work, Bernstein's dramas are dismissed largely because of the author's gender: "What this highly talented playwright lacks (and this we must assume to be a characteristically female shortcoming) is that concentrated intellect . . . without which a truly dramatic effect cannot occur" (691).

While there can be no question that Bernstein's female-ness had a considerable and lasting effect on her recep-tion, her reception as a Jewish author in Germany is less clear-cut. Her Jewish background is not a factor in any of her early reviews; the bulk of her literary activity occurred twenty-three years before Hitler came to power. She re-mained highly regarded in Munich's literary circles even at the point in time when it became dangerous to associate with Jews. There is no evidence that her works were burned or banned during the Third Reich: *Kingly Children* was performed on German stages as late as 1943—one year after the author's deportation to Theresienstadt. The attack on her during the Nazi era was directed more at the author than at her works: she and Gabriele were evicted from their apartment and thus forced to discontinue the literary salon that had been a meeting place for numerous famous authors and musicians of the era, including Lud-wig Ganghofer, Hugo von Hofmannsthal, Ricarda Huch, Richard Strauss, Rainer Maria Rilke, Gerhart Hauptmann, Theodor Fontane, Ludwig Thoma, Henrik Ibsen, Frank Wedekind, and Thomas Mann (who met his future wife, Katja Pringsheim, through Elsa Bernstein's mediation). Later, after her incarceration in the concentration camp, Bernstein's writing was curbed to such a degree that liter-ary activity became impossible.

Her posthumous reception, until a somewhat erratic Bernstein revival since the 1990s, has been scant, consist-ing of two dissertations devoted to her, in 1923 and 1952 (Wiener; Kriwanek); a few dissertations and articles in which she appears alongside other authors (see Amets-bichler; Emonds; Gleibs; Novak; Pierce); one scholarly monograph, in 1985 (Zophoniasson-Baierl); translations of four of her plays (*Twilight*, trans. Grummann, 1912; *Kingly Children*, trans. Meltzer, 1910; *John Herkner*, trans. Harned, 1911; and *Maria Arndt*, trans. Kord, 1996); and one recent performance—of *Maria Arndt*, in an unpublished translation by Curt Columbus based on Kord's 1996 translation, at the Steppenwolf Theater in Chicago (Feb.–Mar. 2002).

Assimilation and Survival: Elsa Bernstein's Jewishness

Although of Jewish descent, Elsa Bernstein grew up as a devout Protestant and considered herself both a Christian and part of the bourgeois educated elite, the *Bildungsbürgertum*, whose claims to cultural superiority were symbolized in the works of Richard Wagner, among Germany's most anti-Semitic composers. When she, who defined herself as a Protestant Wagnerian, was incarcerated for being a Jew and non-German in 1942, she was accorded VIP status a few weeks after her arrival and transferred from overcrowded barracks to a *Prominentenhaus*, a "house for prominent people." This transfer almost certainly saved her life: as a *Prominente*, Bernstein had privileged status, which meant higher food and water rations, the permission to receive one parcel a month, the permission to write once every eight days, and relative safety (*Prominente* were not included in transports to the East, although there were exceptions to this rule). Only fourteen percent of all Theresienstadt inmates survived—and only four percent of all Jews who were deported east from Theresienstadt. The estimated survival rate among VIPs in the same camp was eighty-four percent. Bernstein received this privileged status through the intervention of Winifred

Wagner, Richard Wagner's daughter-in-law, the woman who made the *Festspiele* in Bayreuth a vehicle of Nazi propaganda, who was close friends with Hitler himself, and who was even rumored to have been a serious marriage possibility for him. Bernstein's life in the concentration camp was thus full of paradox: she frequently and openly expressed her utter disgust with Hitler, but she consorted with National Socialists and Nazi sympathizers and shared their view of Jews as a race rather than a religious community. While her memoirs describe the mass murder of the Jews in no uncertain terms ("ice-cold, calculated mass murder by gas" [*Das Leben* 156]), they are also replete with descriptions of Jewish racial characteristics: she once remarked—in terms she clearly intended to be complimentary—that her husband, Max Bernstein, did not have Jewish features. Even in Theresienstadt, she remained part of the cultural elite: of the 409 lectures that were given during her three years there, two were by her (one on the subject of Christianity). She maintained a safe distance from Jewishness, emphasizing her unfamiliarity with basic Yiddish terms like *treyf*, referring to the people selected for transports as "the Jews," and frequently expressing her fears of having to consort with this "mob" (153). Both Elsa Bernstein and Gerty Spies considered insignificant the relief they experienced due to their VIP status and repeatedly stated this in their respective memoirs. Yet that attitude was belied by Bernstein's experience: VIPs were given not only basic privileges that improved their chances for survival, such as higher food rations, but also treatment that preserved human dignity, such as the right to keep clean. In her Theresienstadt memoirs she writes:

And the water-pipes are working! The john has become a W. C. And in every washroom, a faucet and a drain. Announcement: every Sunday morning we are permitted to heat the boiler in the basement of the washhouse; the ladies will be allowed to do laundry. The gentlemen, as well, if they feel like it, they add by way of a joke. Yes, we're doing well, we VIPs, and it is understandable that the other inhabitants of the ghetto envy us greatly, even hate us somewhat. (*Das Leben* 68)

Incredibly, the VIPs of Theresienstadt even enjoyed occasional cultural events: Bernstein attended cabaret and opera performances while in the camp and kept a personal reader for some of her time there. Both her reviews of these performances and her frequently condescending comments on non-VIP Jews indicate clearly that she identified herself as an upper-class German, saw her classification as Jewish as the ultimate attack on her identity, and sought to defend herself by becoming the center of a culturally elite group. The VIPs of Theresienstadt continued to use titles from their former lives, addressing themselves formally as Professor, Your Excellency, or Countess; non-prominent Jews were not even allowed to visit. While this strategy undoubtedly helped Bernstein survive and daily maintain her dignity—both Spies in *My Years in Theresienstadt* and Ruth Klüger in *Weiter leben* (Still Alive) have described at length the processes of writing to survive and dissociation—it must also have aided the Nazis in their presentation of the camp as a benevolent institution designed only to separate Jews from Germans. Theresienstadt was the site of the Nazi propaganda film *Der Führer gibt den Juden eine Stadt* (The Führer Gives a City to the Jews), whose

Jewish director was deported to Auschwitz immediately after its completion. When Theresienstadt was promoted to the status of concentration camp (from a ghetto), it became a display piece for a Red Cross visit, proving to the international community how magnanimously Hitler's Germany treated Jews—with the help of Jewish artists and musicians who were later murdered in Auschwitz.

Elsa Porges, Elsa Bernstein, Ernst Rosmer, L-126, Obliterated: What's in a Name?

Like many other eighteenth-to-early-twentieth-century women writers, Elsa Bernstein chose a male pseudonym. "Ernst Rosmer," adapted from Henrik Ibsen's *Rosmersholm* (1886), defined her as a disciple of one of the major playwrights of her time and simultaneously allied her with the German naturalist movement, which was centrally indebted to Ibsen's dramatic work. Whereas most other women writers upheld their anonymity or pseudonymity, many throughout their writing careers, Bernstein had her pseudonym dismantled very early, in Schlenther's essay on Bernstein in the 1893 issue of the *Magazin für Litteratur*. His essay marks one of the most significant moments in her career, for the demolition of her disguise (without the author's consent) is clearly the purpose of his essay:

> The lady still calls herself Ernst Rosmer. Her real name, however, will not remain unknown much longer, and when it becomes known, one will search in vain for a second female playwright of comparable power and intensity. Ernst Rosmer or rather (let us end the masquerade!) Frau Elsa Bernstein is, among talented writers, exceptional. (223)

Schlenther, the author of a monograph on Luise Gottsched, who was considered the first German woman playwright, saw the end of Bernstein's masquerade as the beginning of a new literary epoch, one that featured, for the first time, a female dramatist worthy of note. The identity of the famous Ernst Rosmer soon became an open secret: Kerr, in a review of the 1895 performance of *Tedeum*, sarcastically describes Elsa Bernstein's stepping in front of the curtain and taking a bow on behalf of Ernst Rosmer. But the obliteration of Bernstein's pseudonym had an unforeseen effect on her reception: it revealed her gender identity, thus exposing her plays to sexist critique, but it did not result in a link between her work and her personal identity, thus robbing the author of public acknowledgment of her work. Rudolph Lothar's 1905 critique, in which he consistently refers to the author as Frau Rosmer, is a fairly typical example:

> Frau Rosmer can claim with pride that she is the first woman whose dramatic activity has been taken seriously. . . . It is somewhat strange that writing women have so rarely conquered the stage. But this fact can be explained by considering even Frau Rosmer's work. Because they have never obtained economic independence, women lack a sense for the active. Thus they cannot differentiate between activity and action. Frau Rosmer, as well, takes as her point of departure the lyric—of course, without realizing it. She does not know what action is, despite her dramas. Her heroes are all passive in a dramatic sense, even if they do all sorts of things on stage. It is always Woman or, rather, the lyric qualities embodied in Woman that are the determining aspects of her plays.   (165)

Lothar's summary dismissal of Bernstein's dramas as feminine ("Frau Rosmer's feminine nature is her power and her weakness; she wants us to mistake passivity for action" [167]) is both the consequence of and answer to Schlenther's triumphant unveiling of the new female voice in naturalist drama. It also demonstrates the dilemma in which most women writers of the age found themselves: when writing, particularly writing for the stage, was considered unfeminine, a pseudonym offered the possibility to become known as an author while remaining unknown as a person. Lothar's critique perverts both these aspects into their opposites: while presenting Bernstein's gender as a handicap for her work, it continues to withhold from the author, in its perfidious renaming of her as Frau Rosmer, the acknowledgment for her work that other women writers obtained by relinquishing their gender anonymity.

The proliferation of names coupled with the inability to determine one's own name can be interpreted as one of the most defining aspects of a subjugated person (or people). Barbara Hahn forcefully makes this point in her analysis of the naming and renaming of Jews during the Third Reich: Jewish men were forced to assume "Israel" and Jewish women "Sara" as a middle name so they could be instantly identified as Jews. Literary history has shown that major male writers are usually identified by a single name (Goethe, Schiller, Lessing, etc.) whereas the names of women writers are legion (e.g., Caroline Dorothea Albertine Schlegel-Schelling, née Michaelis, formerly Schlegel, widowed Böhmer; or the 21 pseudonyms of Katharina [Kathinka] Rosa Therese Pauline Modesta Zitz-Halein).

The plethora of names for women writers (maiden names; married names; divorce names; double names; and often several pseudonyms, both male and female) and the uncertainty about how to designate the author (with the name of her first husband? the name of her last husband? the name under which she wrote the most? the name under which she became most famous?) has undoubtedly affected the reception of women writers until deep into the twentieth century. The naming difficulty has also affected the availability of biographical information, the availability of women's texts, and the canonization of women's works throughout literary history.

Bernstein's names can thus be seen as a mark of inferiority—of author or of person—and as a means of obliterating Bernstein—as author or as person—several times throughout her life. To avoid the common assumption that women make poor playwrights, she chose a male pseudonym before embarking on her writing career. In reviews, her pseudonym was revoked, without her consent, to enable the gendered critique of her plays. In Theresienstadt, her name was replaced by a designation: L-126, Kategorie A, Prominent. And in death, her name was finally obliterated: Elsa Bernstein's urn was buried in her father's grave; their common tombstone lists only one name: Heinrich Porges.

About the Play

Twilight, written at a time when women were still barred from German universities, features the first female doctor to enter the German stage—a daring feat even given the iconoclasm of contemporary drama. Sabine Graef is a highly competent ophthalmologist who is called in to treat Isolde Ritter and in so doing must face the prejudices of Isolde's father against educated women. The composer Heinrich Ritter considers university study for women "modern nonsense" and women in general mentally retarded: "How can such a petticoat have any sense? A thimbleful of sense—at the most." When Sabine proves otherwise through her competent treatment of his daughter, Ritter and Sabine fall in love. Their affair begins her slow slide into conformity with Ritter's ideas of femininity: "Don't make such a wise face. It suits you so much better to look a little frightened, and dumb." Sabine takes voice lessons from him and allows him to tyrannize her until little is left of her self-confidence. When she is offered a prestigious research position in Berlin, he proposes marriage, to which she reacts by fainting with joy and which she accepts, filled with "nameless bliss," after he has assured her that she is "good enough" for him. With the nameless bliss, she experiences a lethargy that permits her to give up her vocation in medicine and let herself be forced, even beaten, into marriage:

> RITTER: Isn't this a thousand times better than the whole shabby medical travesty you've been playing?
> SABINE (*her head at his shoulder*): Better—yes, it is.
> RITTER: I will teach you to be happy. You will be spanked if you're not happy. And I will cure you of your cleverness.
> SABINE: I want to become stupid—very happily stupid.

It seems that this is the happy ending the play prepares us for: Sabine giving up her job—"My bride is a lady, not a doctor"—and submitting to Heinrich as both her husband and her teacher of music: "You have much to learn, my child. And now keep time: one, two—one, two—"

The wedded bliss fails because of the daughter's jealousy. Isolde, who throughout the play makes every effort to keep her father with her, finally succeeds when she attempts suicide and goes blind in the process. On the day before her departure for Berlin, Sabine makes one last effort to save her love: she pleads with Ritter to take her into his house as an unpaid housekeeper, without marrying her. "I will give up my job. Everything. I will go with you and take care of her [Isolde]. I will want nothing for myself. I will be so economical. I will do everything she asks. Just let me be with you. Just let me be with you." Ritter refuses her offer, because he foresees that this is an arrangement that Isolde would be unable to live with.

Twilight is, to my knowledge, the first play written in Germany that takes seriously women's capacity for university education and professional vocation, but it nonetheless clearly juxtaposes, in the play's conclusion, woman's professionalism and intellectualism with domestic happiness. At the beginning of the play, Sabine is portrayed as competent, universally respected, an expert in her field—but not as happy. She considers her vocation not as a source of contentment but exclusively as a service to others that demands the sacrifice of her own happiness and wishes. The final scene makes abundantly clear that happiness to her would have meant marriage to Ritter, an arrangement that would have forced her to become "happily stupid." For Sabine, the tragedy at the end of the play is her forced return to the medical profession after she has known the "nameless bliss" of her affair with Ritter.

The author's rather crass wording "happily stupid" can be read not as an expression of sarcasm but as a fair description of the female dilemma in the 1890s: in the world portrayed in *Twilight*, a woman can be educated or married, intelligent or happy, but not both. It does not take much imagination to picture how a female spectator, possibly a woman who was considering emigration to Switzerland or the United States to obtain a university education, might have been affected by a performance of this play.

The play is rife with clearly autobiographical connections, which should be noted but resisted as a basis for an interpretation of the play. Isolde in *Twilight* is, like Elsa Bernstein, the daughter of a renowned composer and Wagner enthusiast who moved from Vienna to Munich. Both men share the same first name—Heinrich—and Heinrich Ritter's love of Liszt could be read as an allusion to the persistent rumor that Heinrich Porges, Bernstein's father, was an illegitimate son of that composer. Isolde's decidedly Wagnerian first name—we are led to believe that she was named after the heroine of *Tristan und Isolde*—is easily decipherable as an allusion to the author's own first name: Elsa is another notable heroine from a Wagner opera, *Lohengrin*. And like Isolde, Elsa Bernstein had a severe eye disease as a young girl that forced her to take to her bed for a number of years and finally left her completely blind around 1920. Even the names of the characters in the play can be read in rather obvious terms: by his name Heinrich Ritter (*Ritter* is "knight") is defined both as a character from a distant, mythical past—witness his conversation with Sabine, in which he idolizes the Middle Ages—and as someone who at first gallantly, in the end forcibly, spends his life in the service of Isolde, the Wagnerian damsel in distress. These hints notwithstanding, the autobiographical aspects of the play should be taken not as an allusion to Bernstein's life and family but rather as part of the play's aesthetic approach. Two aspects of naturalist drama may help us read the autobiographical allusions throughout the play in a different manner: first, the naturalist theory that art and literature should depict every appearance of the subject exactly as it is found in nature; second, the naturalist belief that heredity and environment play a crucial part in character development.

One of the most pervasive themes in German naturalism is the relation between art and nature, more specifically art (esp. literature) and the natural sciences. Scientific and technological progress was one of the most defining aspects of the second half of the nineteenth century, and to some extent this progress resulted in the questioning of the relevance of art and also of literature. The natural sciences sought to explain the world through applications of natural law and discoveries of cause and effect: Charles Darwin, in *Origin of Species* (1859) and *The Descent of Man* (1871), laid the foundation for later works on heredity and environment as central factors in the evolution of any, including the human, species. Hippolyte Taine developed, in the newly established discipline of sociology, a thesis that would become central for naturalist thought: that humans are determined by their *race* (genetic heritage), their *temps* (historical era) and their *milieu* (social circumstance). In order to safeguard the relevance of the arts in a time of scientific discovery, the naturalists sought to integrate scientific methods and approaches into art and literature—a programmatic tendency that later became known as the *Verwissenschaftlichung der Kunst* (the scientification of art). In his book *Die naturwissenschaftlichen Grundlagen der Poesie* (1887; The Scientific Foundation of Poetry), Wilhelm Bölsche redefines authors as experimenters and their work as a "poetic experiment," an aspect that he saw as central and defining for naturalist writing (8). Thus art becomes science; the artist becomes a scientist; and the business of art and literature now is to provide an objective and realistic view of human life, to analyze human beings and the human condition in the same detached manner as a biologist would analyze bacteria under a microscope.

Bernstein's drama *Twilight* can be read, as Astrid Weigert has already done, both as an exemplification of naturalist theory and as a rather critical commentary on one of its central tenets, the treatment of art as science. That the play presents, in reverse gender constellation, a male artist (Ritter) and a female scientist (Sabine) makes explicit a problem that does not appear in the naturalist debate on art and science but still plays an important part in that debate: women were not permitted to attend German universities, and science around the turn of the century was an exclusively male domain. Thus the naturalist call for the scientification of art can, as Weigert has pointed out, be indirectly understood as a call for the masculinization of art.

Dr. Sabine Graef's discipline, medicine, figures prominently in naturalist aesthetics, which purported—for example, in the theories of Emile Zola (*"Experimental Novel"* and *Thérèse Raquin*), that both medical doctors and literary authors based their work on exact observation, diagnosis, and experimentation. Isolde's visual impairment and ultimate blindness and Dr. Graef's profession as ophthamologist and eye surgeon can both be seen as commentaries on naturalist aesthetics, in which seeing and observing form the basis for recognizing the truth. The play's title connotes limitation of vision and vagueness, which stand in stark contrast to the naturalist desire for precision of vision. It is no accident that Dr. Graef, despite her strictly scientific demeanor and her obvious competence, is unable to determine the cause of Isolde's illness. While observation, analysis, and diagnosis are part of her work, they do not constitute its ultimate purpose. She criticizes the highly experimental treatment to which Isolde was subjected before her arrival (the mercury injections) and ultimately offers her services as an unpaid nurse—that is, she is willing to reduce herself to a medical existence that places the emphasis on healing and caretaking rather than on diagnosis, experimentation, research, and treatment.

Heinrich Ritter, the play's artist, represents Dr. Graef's opposite not only in the art-science debate but also in another debate among naturalists, who considered themselves proponents of modern art. Enthusiasm for Wagner and Liszt characterizes Ritter as part of the old school. He is uncomfortable with modern music and lives in the past; he refers all the important moments in his life—his marriage, his wife's death, Isolde's birth, and the beginning of Isolde's disease—to long-past musical events such as opera premieres. Thus the opposition between Sabine and Ritter is also that between progressive thinking and apathetic nostalgia. As the play develops, it becomes clear that his artistic influence on her is considerably stronger than her scientific influence on him: Ritter, Carl (a family friend), and Isolde all view Sabine's intellectualism as one-sided and criticize her, though she holds a university degree and during the play receives an award for her research, as uneducated in the sense of the German *Bildungsbürgertum*, whose claims to cultural superiority over and contempt for the working members of society are here, interestingly enough, epitomized in Ritter's Wagner enthusiasm. Conversations throughout the play reveal that Sabine has not received the upper-tier bourgeois education that was designed to make girls attractive to men of the same class: a smattering of languages, musical and artistic knowledge, and conversational skills aiming at the entertainment of a prospective suitor. Sabine does not know the works of Wagner and is unfamiliar with standard paintings and sculptures; she does not draw, sing, or play an instrument. Although she subjects herself to just such an education—she takes voice lessons from Ritter—her scientific orientation has little influence on the composer, who remains skeptical toward science in general and medicine in particular to the end of the play, despite Sabine's success in treating Isolde. He is particularly opposed to Sabine's efforts to find the origins of the disease, because they might implicate his conduct (in 1999, a Hamburg ophthamologist, Alexander Bialasiewicz, diagnosed Isolde's disease as described in the play as caused by parental syphilis [Bake and Kiupel 17]). Ritter views her failure to find the cause as proof that science is ultimately unable to explain all aspects of life.

In the final analysis, one could read the play, with Weigert, as a critical commentary on the aesthetic tenets of the naturalist movement, for it seems that Bernstein opposes one of the movement's most central ideas, the scientification of art, as untenable. Both Ritter's refusal of all scientific ideas—even as he profits from them—and the separation of the two central characters at the end of the play point in this direction: Sabine Graef the scientist and Heinrich Ritter the artist coexist at the end of the play as alternatives, but neither learns from the other. Ritter's refusal to adopt Sabine's scientific viewpoint remains adamant to the end. And Sabine's attempts to adapt to the artistic realm (through her voice lessons, her interest in Ritter's music, and her attempt to replace her objective and professional demeanor with more emotive qualities) are rejected unequivocally. Thus Bernstein, while adopting the style and themes of naturalist drama, opposes its aesthetic foundation, for in her dramatic world, science and art remain incompatible.

Note

My translation is indebted to Paul H. Grummann's 1912 translation in three places: Carl's poem (act 2), Ritter's song (act 3), and Isolde's traveling song (act 5) are taken from Grummann. The remainder of the English is mine.

Works Cited and Consulted

Ametsbichler, Elizabeth Graff. "Society, Gender, Politics, and Turn-of-the-Century Theater: Elsa Bernstein (ps. Ernst

Rosmer) and Arthur Schnitzler." Diss. U of Maryland, College Park, 1992.

Arnold, Robert. *Das moderne Drama*. Straßburg: Trübner, 1912. Munich: Beck, 1925.

Bake, Rita, and Birgit Kiupel. "Königskinder im Salon: Zum Leben und Schaffen Elsa Bernsteins alias Ernst Rosmers." Bernstein, *Das Leben* 11–40.

Bartels, Adolf. *Die deutsche Dichtung der Gegenwart: Die Alten und die Jungen*. Leipzig: Avenarius, 1904.

[Bernstein, Elsa]. *Dämmerung: Schauspiel in fünf Akten: Von Ernst Rosmer*. Berlin: Fischer, 1893.

———. *Das Leben als Drama: Erinnerungen an Theresienstadt*. Ed. Rita Bake and Birgit Kiupel. Dortmund: Ebersbach, 1999.

———. *Maria Arndt: A Play in Five Acts*. Trans. Susanne Kord. Kelly 84–107.

———. *Twilight: Drama in Five Acts: By Ernst Rosmer*. Trans. Paul H. Grummann. *Poet Lore* 23 (1912): 369–443.

Bölsche, Wilhelm. *Die naturwissenschaftlichen Grundlagen der Poesie: Prolegomena einer realistischen Ästhetik*. Tübingen: Niemeyer, 1976.

Darwin, Charles. *The Descent of Man, and Selection in Relation to Sex*. Introd. John Tyler Bonner and Robert M. May. Princeton: Princeton UP, 1981.

———. *On the Origin of Species by Means of Natural Selection; or, The Preservation of Favoured Races in the Struggle for Life*. New York: Heritage, 1963.

Emonds, Friederike Bettina. "Gattung und Geschlecht: Inszenierungen des Weiblichen in Dramen deutschsprachiger Theaterschriftstellerinnen." Diss. U of California, Davis, 1993.

Garland, Henry, and Mary Garland. "Elsa Bernstein." *The Oxford Companion to German Literature*. Ed. Garland and Garland. Oxford: Oxford UP, 1997. 80.

Giesing, Michaela. "Theater als verweigerter Raum: Dramatikerinnen der Jahrhundertwende in deutschsprachigen

Ländern." *Frauen—Literatur—Geschichte*. Ed. Hiltrud Gnüg and Renate Möhrmann. Stuttgart: Metzler, 1985. 240–59.

———. "Verhältnisse und Verhinderungen: Deutschsprachige Dramatikerinnen um die Jahrhundertwende." *Frauen—Literatur—Geschichte: Schreibende Frauen vom Mittelalter bis zur Gegenwart*. Ed. Hiltrud Gnüg and Renate Möhrmann. 2nd ed. Stuttgart: Metzler, 1999. 261–78.

Gleibs, Yvonne. "Juden im kulturellen und wissenschaftlichen Leben Münchens in der zweiten Hälfte des 19. Jahrhunderts." Diss. U of Munich, 1981.

Hahn, Barbara. *Unter falschem Namen: Von der schwierigen Autorschaft der Frauen*. Frankfurt: Suhrkamp, 1991.

Hamann, Brigitte. *Winifred Wagner oder Hitlers Bayreuth*. Munich: Piper, 2002.

Kelly, Katherine, ed. *Modern Drama by Women, 1880s–1930s: An International Anthology*. London: Routledge, 1996.

Kerr, Alfred. "Ernst Rosmer." *Das neue Drama: Die Welt im Drama*. Vol. 1. Berlin: Fischer, 1917. 315–18.

———. "Ernst Rosmer: *Königskinder*." *Das neue Drama: Die Welt im Drama*. Vol. 3. Berlin: Fischer, 1917. 166–69.

Klüger, Ruth. *Weiter leben: Eine Jugend*. Göttingen: Wallstein, 1992.

Kord, Susanne. "Bernstein, Elsa (1866–1949)." *Modern Germany: An Encyclopedia of History, People, and Culture, 1871–1990*. Vol. 1. Ed. Dieter K. Buse and Jürgen C. Doerr. New York: Garland, 1998. 102–03.

———. "Elsa Bernstein (Ernst Rosmer), 1866–1949." Kelly 80–83.

———. "Die Gelehrte als Zwitterwesen in Schriften von Autorinnen des 18. und 19. Jahrhunderts." *Querelles: Jahrbuch für Frauenforschung* 1 (1996): 158–89.

Kriwanek, Gerhard. "Das dramatische Werk von Elsa Bernstein." Diss. U of Vienna, 1952.

Lorenz, Dagmar C. G. *Keepers of the Motherland: German Texts by Jewish Women Writers*. Lincoln: U of Nebraska P, 1997.

———. *Verfolgung bis zum Massenmord : Holocaust-Diskurse in deutscher Sprache aus der Sicht der Verfolgten*. New York: Lang, 1992.

Lorenz, Dagmar C. G., and Gabriele Weinberger, eds. *Insiders and Outsiders: Jewish and Gentile Culture in Germany and Austria*. Detroit: Wayne State UP, 1994.

Lothar, Rudolph. *Das deutsche Drama der Gegenwart*. Munich: Müller, 1905.

Novak, Sigrid Gerda Scholtz. "Images of Womanhood in the Works of German Female Dramatists, 1892–1918." Diss. Johns Hopkins U, 1973.

Pierce, Nancy Jean Franklin. "Woman's Place in Turn-of-the-Century Drama: The Function of Female Figures in Selected Plays by Gerhart Hauptmann, Frank Wedekind, Ricarda Huch, and Elsa Bernstein." Diss. U of California, Irvine, 1988.

Schlenther, Paul. *Frau Gottsched und die bürgerliche Komödie: Ein Kulturbild aus der Zopfzeit*. Berlin: Hertz, 1886.

———. "Was kann dich in der Dämmerung so ergreifen?" *Magazin für Litteratur* 62 (1893): 222–23.

Soergel, Albert. *Dichtung und Dichter der Zeit*. 1916. 19th ed. Leipzig: Voigtländer, 1928.

Soergel, Albert, and Curt Hohoff. *Dichtung und Dichter der Zeit*. 2nd ed. Vol. 1. Düsseldorf: Bagel, 1961.

Spies, Gerty. *My Years in Theresienstadt: How One Woman Survived the Holocaust*. Trans. Jutta R. Tragnitz. Amherst: Prometheus, 1997.

Taine, Hippolyte. *Histoire de la littérature anglaise*. 4 vols. Paris: Hachette, 1863–64.

Weigert, Astrid. "Schriftstellerinnen als Ästhetikerinnen in Romantik und Naturalismus am Beispiel von Dorothea Schlegel und Elsa Bernstein." Diss. Georgetown U, 1999.

Wiener, Kurt. "Die Dramen Elsa Bernsteins (Ernst Rosmers)." Diss. U of Vienna, 1923.

Zola, Emile. *"The Experimental Novel" and Other Essays*. New York: Haskell, 1964.

———. *Thérèse Raquin*. Paris: Calmann, 1909.

Zophoniasson-Baierl, Ulrike. *Elsa Bernstein alias Ernst Rosmer: Eine deutsche Dramatikerin im Spannungsfeld der literarischen Strömungen des Wilhelminischen Zeitalters*. Berne: Lang, 1985.

BIBLIOGRAPHY OF BERNSTEIN'S WORKS

In German

"Abschied." Poem. *Jugend* 19 (1914): 1354.

Achill: Tragödie in drei Akten von Ernst Rosmer. Berlin: Fischer, 1910.

"Achtzig Jahre." Poem. Gleibs 236.

"Der Alltag." Poem. Gleibs 235.

"Der alte Baum." Poem. *Jugend* 22 (1917): 522.

"Die alte Frau." Dramatic novella. Unpublished. 1926.

"Aphorismus." Poem. *Das XXVte Jahr.* Berlin: Fischer, 1911. 317.

"April." Poem. *Jugend* 16 (1911): 511.

"August-Mittag." Poem. *Jugend* 11 (1906): 894.

"Bärbel." Poem. Gleibs 235.

"Der Bauer und das Prinzeßchen." Tale. *Neue deutsche Rundschau* 6.1 (1895): 262–73.

"Bernstein, Frau Elsa (Ernst Rosmer)." Autobiographical sketch. *Geistiges und künstlerisches München in Selbstbiographien.* Ed. W. Zils. Munich: Kellerer, 1913. 24–25.

Briefe der Frau Elsa an den Soldaten Franz. Letters dated 1939–42. Ed. F. v. Wesendonk. 2nd ed. Mittenwald, 1977.

"Caprice." Novella. *Magazin für Litteratur* 62 (1893): 14–17.

"Corriger l'amour." Novella. *Madonna* 27–93.

"Dagny: Drama." Manuscript. 1900.

Dämmerung: Schauspiel in fünf Akten: Von Ernst Rosmer. Berlin: Fischer, n.d. [1893].

"Deutsche Ehe." Poem. *Kriegsmappe des SDS.* Ed. Peter Behrend and Richard Dehmel. Berlin: Deutscher Kurier, 1916. 79.

"Der deutsche Sieg." Poem. *Almanach dem Verein für Kinder-Volksküchen und Volks-Kinderhorte e. V. gewidmet von hervorragenden Frauen und Männern Deutschlands.* Berlin: Feyl, 1914. 53.

"Ehe: Drama." Manuscript. 1914.

"Elsa Bernstein (Ernst Rosmer)." Autobiographical sketch. *Bildende Geister: Unsere bedeutendsten Schriftsteller der Gegenwart und Vergangenheit in charakteristischen Selbstbiographien.* Vol. 1. Ed. Fritz Abshoff. Berlin: Oestergaard, 1905. 18.

"England." Poem. *Jugend* 19 (1914): 1068.

"Erblindend." Poem. *Magazin für Litteratur* 21 (1891): 335.

"Erkennung: Komödie." Play in manuscript. N.d.

"Erlebnis." Novella. *Süddeutsche Monatshefte* 26 (1928–29): 3–5.

"Es war einmal." Poem. *Frühlingszeit: Eine Lenzes- und Liebesgabe unsern erwachsenen Töchtern zur Unterhaltung und Erhebung gewidmet von den deutschen Dichterinnen der Gegenwart.* Ed. Bertha von Suttner. Berlin: Globus, 1896. 207–08.

"Euch." Poem. Gleibs 238.

"Die Freundinnen: Komödie." Manuscript. 1909.

"Frühlingsmorgen." Poem. *Licht und Schatten* 3 (1913).

"Dem 'Führer.'" Poem. Dated 3 May 1945. Gleibs 114–15.

Gleibs, Yvonne. "Juden im kulturellen und wissenschaftlichen Leben Münchens in der zweiten Hälfte des 19. Jahrhunderts." Diss. U of Munich, 1981.

"Grabschrift." Poem. Gleibs 238.

"Herbstfäden." Poem. *Jugend* 3 (1898): 148–49.

"Herbstveilchen." Poem. *Jugend* 2 (1897): 709.

"In der Mauernstrasse." Novella. *Madonna* 115–36.

Johannes Herkner: Schauspiel von Elsa Porges (Ernst Rosmer). Berlin: Fischer, 1904.

"Johannes Kepler: Drama." Manuscript. 1926.

"Kletten im Garten." Poem. Gleibs 237.

Königskinder: Ein deutsches Märchen in drei Akten von Ernst Rosmer. Berlin: Fischer, 1894.

"Kummer." Poem. Gleibs 236–37.

Das Leben als Drama: Erinnerungen an Theresienstadt. Dortmund: Ebersbach, 1999.

Letters to Hermann Beuttemüller (dictations taken by Gabriele Porges), from 1 Aug. 1908 to 9 Dec. 1929. Deutsches Literaturarchiv/Schiller-Nationalmuseum, Marbach a. N.

Letters to Hermann Sudermann, from 21 Feb. 1902 to 25 Sept. 1927. Deutsches Literaturarchiv/Schiller-Nationalmuseum, Marbach a. N. (Cotta-Archiv).

"La Madeleine." Poem. *Jugend* 17 (1912): 1599.

"Madonna." Novella. *Madonna* 5–24.

Madonna: Novellen: Von Ernst Rosmer. Berlin: Fischer, 1894.

"Mädchensommer." Poem. *Jugend* 3 (1898): 360.

Mädchensommer: Für eine Singstimme und Pianoforte (op. 80). Augsburg: Böhn, 1913.

"Das Märchen vom Leid." Tale. *Meisternovellen deutscher Frauen.* Vol. 1. Ed. Ernst Brausewetter. Leipzig: Fock, 1907. 289–99. *Im Nonnengarten: An Anthology of German Women's Writing, 1850–1907.* Ed. Michelle Stott and Joseph O. Baker. Prospect Heights: Waveland, 1997. 331–39.

"März." Poem. *Jugend* 10 (1905): 219.

Maria Arndt: Schauspiel in fünf Akten von Ernst Rosmer. Berlin: Fischer, 1908.

"Merete: Schauspiel." Manuscript. 1902.

"Michel." Novella. Manuscript. Ca. 1913.

"Milost Pan." Novella. *Madonna* 139–73.

"Eine Mutter." Poem. *Deutsche Dichtung* 13 (1892–93): 161.

Mutter Maria: Ein Totengedicht in fünf Wandlungen von Ernst Rosmer. Berlin: Fischer, 1900.

Nausikaa: Tragödie von Ernst Rosmer. Berlin: Fischer, 1906.

"Neugriechisches Volkslied von der Insel Karpathes, deutsch von Ernst Rosmer." Song translation. *Licht und Schatten: Wochenschrift für Schwarzweisskunst und Dichtung* 1.3 (1910).

"Notre Dame." Poem. *Licht und Schatten* 3 (1913).

"Platonisch." Novella. *Madonna* 95–113.

"Requiem: Eine Phantasie." Manuscript. 1922.

Schicksal: Schauspiel. Berlin, 1919.

"Der Schwester." Poem excerpts. *An den Wind geschrieben: Lyrik der Freiheit.* Ed. Manfred Schlösser. 2nd ed. Darmstadt: Agora, 1961. 197.

"Sonett." Poem. Gleibs 237.

"Sprüche." Poem. *Jugend* 3 (1898): 190, 272.

Tedeum: Gemütskomödie in fünf Akten: Von Ernst Rosmer. Berlin: Fischer, 1896.

Themistokles: Tragödie in fünf Akten: Von Ernst Rosmer. Berlin: Fischer, 1897.

"Der Todesritt." Poem. *Deutsche Dichtung* 14 (1893): 287–88.

"Vierzeiler." Poem. Gleibs 238.

"Vorfrühling." Poem. *Jugend* 18 (1913): 358.

"Wieland der Schmied." Poem. *Süddeutsche Monatshefte* 12 (1914): 441.

"Winterwald." Poem. *Eine deutsche Kunstspende.* Ed. Otto Julius Bierbaum. Munich: Müller, 1916. 166.

Wir Drei: Fünf Akte: Von Ernst Rosmer. Munich: Schuster, n.d. [1893].

In English Translation

John Herkner. Trans. Mary Harned. *Poet Lore* 22. Boston: Badger, 1911.

Kingly Children: Opera by Humperdinck. Trans. Charles Henry Meltzer. New York: Rullman, 1910.

King's Children, a German Fairy Tale, in Three Acts, by Ernst Rosmer. New York: Rosenfield, n.d.

The King's Children: Retold by J. Walker McSpadden. Stories from Great Operas. New York: Crowell, 1925. 131–49.

Maria Arndt: A Play in Five Acts. Trans. Susanne Kord. *Modern Drama by Women: An International Anthology.* Ed. Katherine Kelly. London: Routledge, 1996. 84–107.

The Royal Children: A Fairy Tale Founded on the Opera: Told for Children by A. A. Chapin. New York: Harper, 1911.

Twilight: Drama in Five Acts. Trans. Paul H. Grummann. *Poet Lore* 23 (1912): 369–443. Poet Lore ser. 2. Boston: Badger, 1917.

NOTE ON THE
MEDICAL TERMS USED IN THE PLAY

- Atropine and eserine are both ophthalmic medications. Atropine dilates the pupil, and eserine constricts it. Both are still used in ophthamology today; atropine is used before and after retinal surgery or for patients with iritis. Eserine is more rarely used and only for patients who have been diagnosed with glaucoma.
- Tuberculosis of the eye was commonly diagnosed throughout the nineteenth and early twentieth centuries.
- Iritis is an intraocular inflammation.
- Superior iridectomy is a form of eye surgery during which an incision is made in the top part of the iris. In the past, this kind of surgery was frequently performed to treat glaucoma and inflammation.
- A coloboma is a hole in the iris, in the play caused by the iridectomy performed on Isolde.
- The sphincter in the eye is the muscle that controls the movement of the pupil.
- Syphilis does not typically cause glaucoma, but it can. One manifestation of it is the appearance of ulcers. Syphilis in the eye can be caused congenitally, meaning the father might pass the disease on to the mother and

the mother to the child. Many children with congenital syphilis have other deformities, such as tooth deformities, hearing difficulties, or mental retardation. Syphilis can also be caused by father-daughter incest. Eye inflammation is more common in this case than in the congenital form.

• Mercury injections, before the advent of effective antibiotics or steroids, were a common treatment in the past, particularly for syphilis. Due to the extreme toxicity of mercury, this treatment is no longer in use.

ELSA BERNSTEIN

Twilight

Characters

Heinrich Ritter
Isolde, his daughter
Sabine Graef
Carl Curtius
Baba, a cook
Anna, a housemaid
A child

ACT I

A large room, not particularly deep, on the ground floor. The middle wall, consisting of a sliding door, leads to Isolde's bedroom. A large glass door to the right, in front, leads through the veranda into the garden. A large window at the right in the rear. Two single-paneled doors on the left. The front one of these leads into Ritter's bedroom, the other into the hallway. Between the two doors, against the wall, a comfortable sofa; above it, a photograph of Beethoven. Oval table and high-backed chairs. On the table is an open red portfolio containing photographs, Schwind's Seven Ravens. *A hanging lamp with an adjustable green shade. To the right, in the corner between the door leading to the hallway and the sliding door, is a serving table with wine bottles, glasses, a basket with baked goods. To the left, in the corner between the sliding door and the window, a gentleman's desk, placed diagonally. Above it, a crayon portrait of Isolde. Between the window and the glass door, a piano with a small bust of Wagner, scattered books and notes. All the furniture is made of dull-brown mahogany, old-fashioned but tasteful and comfortable. The armchairs and the sofa are covered with reddish-brown rep. — The glass door is almost closed. On the windowpanes, a little reddish*

5

evening light that soon disappears. It is twilight. Isolde sits in the armchair next to the table, her feet on a footstool, her head leaning to one side, her shoulders drawn together. Her eyes are closed. In her lap is a blue pair of eyeglasses. Long blond braids bound with light-blue ribbons. A white summer dress. She moves her head repeatedly, restlessly, from side to side, presses her hand against her left temple and groans.

ANNA (*entering from the hallway. White cap and apron. She is carrying plates, tablecloth, and cutlery on a tray, which she places on the serving table. She pulls down the hanging lamp and lights a match*)

ISOLDE (*covering her eyes protectively with both hands*): Don't—don't!

ANNA (*startled, blows out the match*): Oh, yes, well! Thought the miss had turned th' other way.

ISOLDE: Why don't you say something before you light it! This is how I'm supposed to get better!

ANNA: Want to set table for dinner. Herr Ritter must very soon be coming home.

ISOLDE: I don't want a light on. You'll be able to do it in this light, that bit of table setting. After all, it is still bright outside . . . terribly bright. (*She puts on her glasses.*)

ANNA (*secretly glancing at her as she is putting the photographs into the portfolio*): The miss has been looking at pitchers again. With sick eye. Silly pitchers. Herr Ritter should burn all pitchers. Whole pile.

ISOLDE: That's ridiculous! It doesn't hurt me to look. Not at all. Take them away.

ANNA (*pointing at Ritter's door*): There?

ISOLDE (*vehemently*): God, how stupid! Of course! Where else? Certainly not to the pantry!

ANNA (*takes the portfolio into Ritter's room*)

ISOLDE (*takes off her glasses, carefully dabs her left eyelid with her handkerchief, as if wiping away tears, and slowly blows her nose*)

ANNA (*returns; as she is beginning to set the table, slyly*): Should I tell Herr Ritter about looking at pitchers?

ISOLDE: Oh . . . none of Papa's business. Chatterbox. (*Presses her hand to her forehead.*) Headache. Terrible headache.

ANNA (*with sly concern*): Eye headache?

ISOLDE (*breathing heavily but short of breath, blows her nose again*)

ANNA: Miss has a cold, again. Nose weeps. Nose tears.

ISOLDE (*with an effort*): Anna—it's on the night table— bring me—give me the atropine.

ANNA (*putting down the plates in her hand on the table, with a cry*): Is it already! Adropine! Is it left eye?

ISOLDE: Don't yell like that—it hurts my head—you know I can't stand it, the yelling. Well, yes, a bit—the left. Bring me—the atropine, and the dropper—it's in the drawer.

ANNA (*on her way*): Pitchers! And such dark ones! At least if had been nice-colored Emperor Joseph like in our kitchen! Hhhhhh—pitchers! (*Pulling apart the double doors in the middle to step through.*)

ISOLDE (*looking after her, irritated*): Know-it-all. You all know better than I. Now it's the pictures again. It comes if it pleases, or not. Insufferable!

ANNA (*returns with a small brown medicine bottle and a dropper in her hand*): Still is good?

ISOLDE: When—when was it filled last?

ANNA: Was made last time when last big inflammation was of Missy's eye.

ISOLDE: How many weeks ago—

ANNA: Were—weeks—eight. I think. When Mrs. Grandmama had sent cakes from Vienna. Yes—eight. Cakes all already gone.

ISOLDE (*with the bottle in her hand*): I think it is still good . . . give me a fresh handkerchief—white—not a colored one.

ANNA: But surely is only left eye?

ISOLDE (*has opened the bottle, put the dropper in, and removed it again, pressing a few drops out of it to check*): The left—yes.

ANNA: And really bad? Like on Holy Christchildnight? Or just like last time?

ISOLDE (*turns away from her, pulls apart the lids of her left eye with the third and fourth finger of her left hand and puts a single drop in*): Just like last time. (*Leans back with her eyes closed.*)

ANNA: Is better—after dropine?

ISOLDE: It's supposed to be better already? I just took it. (*She feels her eye with the second and third finger of her left hand.*) Don't know—the eye is so hard—and there's pressure.

ANNA (*not without a certain pleasure*): Burns badly, and stings? Phew!

ISOLDE: You're killing me with all your questions! I'm in pain and I'm supposed to give lectures on it. I'm supposed to talk on top of everything else! The handkerchief—take it away—(*gives her the bottle and the dropper*) and—make my bed for me.

ANNA: Jeeze! To bed! That bad!

ISOLDE (*vehemently*): No—it's not bad at all. I am still permitted to take a nap, aren't I? And the handkerchief! The handkerchief.

ANNA (*runs into the bedroom*)

ISOLDE (*pressing her hollow hand over her left eye*): Oh—oh! (*Bursts into tears.*) Will it never stop—ever!

ANNA (*comes back with a handkerchief*): Is it . . .

ISOLDE (*suppresses a sob*)

ANNA (*after a silence of a few seconds*): Miss want to send
for professor.

ISOLDE: No.

ANNA: Only because of calm down Herr Papa. Will be
upset terribly.

ISOLDE: Especially because of Papa, I don't want it. He'll
be much more upset if the doctor is here. I'll tell
him it's only a bit infected and will be better tomorrow . . .

ANNA: But will not be better tomorrow and doctor must
come tomorrow. Is like that with tomorrow every
time. I'll send.

ISOLDE (*half rising*): And I don't want you— (*Sinking back
in pain, from between clenched teeth.*) Yes. All right.

ANNA (*runs out through the front door*)

ISOLDE (*sits silently in the armchair, her glasses covering her
closed eyes, occasionally emitting a slight sound of pain
without opening her lips*)

*Quick steps coming up the stone stairs. Ritter opens the glass
door and enters. Tall slender build, casual movements, distinguished but not elegant. Small head, dark-brown hair, long and
combed back. Clean-shaven, youthful. Gray summer suit, pulled-
down collar with a small black cravat, straw hat in his hand, a
few books under his arm, which he puts down on the piano.*

RITTER: Darling! Hello! (*Cheerfully walks toward her.*) How
are you?

ISOLDE: Thanks—well.

RITTER: Dark? On purpose?

ISOLDE: Oh, it is so—I like it better this way. I can't do anything anyway with the lamp on.

RITTER (*taking her hand and stroking his cheek with it*): Well, don't you have anything to say? What a nice clean shave I have. No more scratchiness. Fantastic! (*Takes a step forward and stumbles over the footstool from which Isolde has removed her feet.*) Hell and damnation—now who could be so idiotic—

ISOLDE: The footstool, Papa—you stumble over that every time.

RITTER (*standing at the table, pulls a matchbox out of his pocket*): Turn around, Bonni. Right around. One could—I want to light a match—I'll keep it very low at first. The place is a death trap!

ISOLDE (*covers her eyes first with her handkerchief, then with both hands, and turns away from the lamp*): But really low.

RITTER (*lights the match, throws it onto the ground, and puts it out with his foot. Pulling at the green lampshade*): Like this? Further away?

ISOLDE: Where have you been? Tell me.

RITTER (*spreads his legs and pulls his arms up*): Such a heat in town! Such heat! And dust! Such a big city is simply brutal. Wipe it out! Just wipe it out.

ISOLDE: Did you go to the post office?

RITTER: Yes—of course—I picked it up and had it changed immediately. The exchange rate fell again, of Austrian marks. Useless money.

ISOLDE: And then? Tell me!

RITTER: Hm . . . right. Guess who I ran into? Czermak from the Grand Opera—you know him. He's supposedly here as a guest star—as Lohengrin and Tannhäuser—him! The higher the C, the dumber the singer. In Vienna he wouldn't even get the part and here he wants to guest-star in it. Do you remember how he spoiled the beautiful solo in the *Te Deum*? Such a beast of a tenor!

ISOLDE: Did he tell you anything—about Vienna?

RITTER: Theater gossip—theater people, what a bunch they are—the musicians are squabbling—over the conductorship of the society concerts—they still don't have a new conductor—(*he stops abruptly and rummages in his back pocket*). I've brought you something—that is, if I didn't sit on it in the horse carriage—at the Victory Gate I just managed to catch it, and because it was already so late—(*he pulls out a squashed package, with a desolate expression*). Oh, darn—I sat on it.

ISOLDE: You're so silly! What is it?

RITTER (*gives it to her*): Perhaps it's still edible—Pisching cake.

ISOLDE: Papa!! Who would ever buy Pisching cake here? You know it's only good in Vienna! A Viennese specialty! Especially since the bakeries here are so bad anyway.

RITTER: But the apothecary shops are better. And since we buy more from them—try it! Maybe it isn't even that bad. (*He walks up and down the room a few times, his hands in his pants pockets. Lost in thought.*) Yes, the society concerts—(*he opens the glass door*). Air! Ah! (*Breathes in deeply, his coat thrown back, his thumbs stuck in the sleeve holes of his vest.*) It's coming in cool from the garden. Well, Bonni, what kind of fellow am I? What kind of papa? Wasn't it a good idea to rent the apartment out here?

ISOLDE: Yes—only the bathroom is too small.

RITTER: We don't take baths that often.

ISOLDE: You don't.

RITTER: I am not that dirty that I always have to be sitting in the water. Dirty. I am never dirty. Today I've already washed my hands twice. After eating, with warm water!

ISOLDE (*forcing herself to smile*): Fabulous! Then surely the world will come to an end soon. I can't believe it.

RITTER (*runs to her, pushes both hands toward her*): There you are—white as snow. Smell them.

13

ISOLDE (*without really looking, but still trying to appear noncha-lant*): Gray—you should wash them again.

RITTER (*looking at his hands*): Again? Three times? No. Now they can wait till tomorrow. Maybe I'll clean my nails again—for you. (*Pulls out his penknife and cleans his nails with the smallest blade.*)

ISOLDE (*fidgeting nervously in her chair, shivering slightly*): There—there is a draft.

RITTER (*surprised*): A draft? But how? Where?

ISOLDE (*stubbornly*): There is a draft.

RITTER (*closing the door again, patiently*): If you say so—to be sure, I don't know. I stopped by at Carl's on the way home. At his new apartment. He wasn't home. I left him a note to ask him to stop by this evening.

ISOLDE: Today—of all days.

RITTER: But he visits almost every day.

ANNA (*comes in through the front door and goes into Isolde's bedroom*): Good evening, Herr Ritter.

RITTER (*without turning around*): Evening. (*To Isolde.*) And because he wasn't there this afternoon—I didn't invite him for my sake.

ISOLDE: He's boring. And stupid.

RITTER: Stupid, stupid, stupid! Carl isn't stupid at all! You get along very well with him.

ISOLDE: Sometimes—but on command—when one has to—

RITTER: Isolde, that is an affectation. To have to. You never have to. And Carl—as if he wasn't like a brother to you! Nonsense.

ANNA (*half opening the door*): Miss—

ISOLDE: Yes. (*To Ritter.*) Papa—but you mustn't be angry—I'm going to bed now. (*Rises with effort.*)

RITTER: Now?

ISOLDE: I don't know—I think—I—I am tired.

RITTER: Bonni—there is something—tired—now—and no light when I came in—(*almost screaming*) your eyes?

ISOLDE (*doesn't answer at first*)

RITTER (*in terrible fear*): Bonni—your eyes?

ISOLDE: Oh Papa—if you're this upset—

RITTER: I'm not upset, not at all—tell me, child—I'm really not upset—an inflammation? Again?

ISOLDE: Just a little—I'm not in pain—not at all—

RITTER (*sad and incredulous*): You're lying to me—I can see it.

ISOLDE: No, Papa—really—it is so slight—and it will be over so quickly—tomorrow.

RITTER (*silently, stands bowed over a little, then very gently and in a lower voice than previously*): My poor poor poor child . . . have you sent for Berger (*he strokes her hair gently*).

ISOLDE: Yes. We sent the groundskeeper for him.

RITTER: Can't I do anything for you? Get something? From the apothecary?

ISOLDE: No. I have atropine. And I have to lie down.

RITTER (*puts his arm around her waist and leads her very slowly toward the bedroom*): Bonni—my only precious child—don't be angry—I don't want to torture you with questions—just tell me yes or no—is it in the iris? Or in the cornea? Is it dangerous?

ISOLDE: I don't know—maybe—

RITTER: If only there are no new growths! What do you think?

ISOLDE: But Papa, you are terrible. How am I supposed to know! Growths—yes—no—I don't know.

RITTER (*alarmed*): Don't get upset—above all, don't get upset. Forgive me. I am so afraid . . . be a good child now.

ISOLDE (*stops walking and leans into his arms*): My poor little Papakins. It doesn't bother me. I'm already used to it.

RITTER (*biting his lips*): Nice thing to get used to. I wish I had this.

ISOLDE (*with a hint of a smile in her voice*): You silly Papa— you would scream! You're such a whiner!

RITTER: Why don't you scream! Kick your feet! Hit something!

ISOLDE: I can't scream. (*She enters the bedroom.*)

RITTER: I'll come see you when you're in bed. (*Closes the door behind her. He takes a few steps toward the front, draws all ten fingers through his hair, sighs deeply. He puts a desk light on and picks up a score. He reconsiders, puts it away, goes to the front door and rings the electric bell right next to it. His hands on his back, he walks nervously up and down, repeatedly stopping and listening at the bedroom door.*)

BABA (*comes in, sturdy woman of fifty-eight with a white, closely tufted head kerchief, colored blouse, and big white apron*): Good evening—

RITTER (*interrupting her*): When did the groundskeeper leave?

BABA: Maybe a quarter hour.

RITTER (*looking at his watch, calculating*): Seven thirty—a quarter to . . . (*he puts his watch away, sighing*). What's for dinner?

BABA: Gosling with rice. Very good.

RITTER (*not raising his voice, but yelling at her, upset and angry*): Have you lost your mind? Such indigestible stuff? With Miss Isolde sick in bed?

BABA: Cook it this morning, I did, and not know—

RITTER: I've told you one hundred times, in the evenings I want light meals, easily digestible. You could talk yourself blue in the face. Womenfolk! Womenfolk!

BABA: But I thought, I did—

RITTER: You're not supposed to think. Nothing but idiocy comes of it when you do.

BABA: I've so much stuff in my head . . .

RITTER: Shoe polish is what you've got in your head! We need something else for Isolde . . .

BABA: If Herr Ritter will just be nice again—I'll roast a chicken for Miss Isolde and for Herr Ritter, I'll—

RITTER (*already mollified*): All right—for God's sake, I'll eat your damn gosling. (*He goes to the glass door, opens it, and steps out onto the stairs.*)

ANNA (*comes out of the bedroom*)

BABA (*addressing Anna, pointing at the bedroom door*): Is bad—very? Herr Ritter is much upset.

ANNA: Is he yelling?

BABA: Yes—idiotic shoe polish and then he's nice again. Oh, Mary and Joseph—I no mind if he yells at me all day long—is still a good man, he is. (*She turns to go. The doorbell rings.*) I open. (*Exits.*)

ANNA (*goes to Ritter*)

RITTER (*hearing her, turns around and hastily enters*): Should I go inside?

ANNA: Herr Ritter should please wait. Miss will ring later.

RITTER: Does she have everything she needs? The chamois pillow? Handkerchiefs? Nothing missing?

ANNA: Nothin' missin'. (*Exits.*)

RITTER (*looking again at his watch*): The devil take these long distances . . .

ANNA (*opens the front door and runs into Carl as he enters*)

CARL (*of medium height, stocky build, with a cumbersome gait, swinging his hips slightly. Open face, big mouth, dreamy eyes. Straight hair parted sideways, hint of a mustache, dressed well but not elegantly. Deep voice and deliberate speech*): Good evening, Herr Ritter.

RITTER (*walking to him*): My dear boy, now I've dragged you out here all for nothing—unfortunately—another iritis.

CARL: She has taken to her bed? Baba told me—is it bad?

RITTER: I know nothing at all. Berger hasn't been here yet. Takes ages till a doctor finally comes. And I'm not allowed to ask her. That annoys her, makes her nervous. I could explode. But do sit down—sit down! Explode!

CARL (*sits down, slowly and expansively, in an armchair, swallows a few times as if trying to say something, licks his lips several times*): Well!!! (*Pause.*)

RITTER: Well—let's talk of something else. What are you doing? You moved out on your shoemaker, didn't you? Why?

CARL: Hmmm . . . The room was nice and quite cheap—thirty marks, breakfast included—but I always had to go through my landlord and landlady's bedroom

to enter it. During the day that was no problem—
but at night—a shoemaker's wife as a Venus with
braids—in her nightgown—hmmm—

RITTER (*half smiling*): Quite a dissonance . . . especially if
you've spent all day studying Raphael's madonnas.

CARL: And on top of all that—company in bed.

RITTER (*in comical shock*): The lady in her nightgown?

CARL: God forbid—not that bad—bedbugs.

RITTER (*shuddering*): Phew! Awful! I always thought they
only existed in Austria.

CARL: Every night, they had a soiree and a ball on top of
me. The entire bedbug aristocracy. And I am not at
all a sociable person. It finally became too much for
me. So I beat it.

RITTER: And your shoemaker and his wife?

CARL: Are crying after me. They said they had never had
such a solid young man in their . . .

RITTER (*has got up to listen at Isolde's door. Turns around
again*): Nothing. I thought I heard her ring the bell.

CARL: I only want to know what the doctor says—otherwise, I wouldn't . . .

RITTER: My dear boy, you are doing me the greatest favor
imaginable. It is difficult not to fret when one is
alone. Especially at such moments—and I am alone
so often. You will dine with me—if you can stom-

ach gosling. Gosling for dinner—Baba's idea. Servants and their brains!

CARL (*licking his lips*): Baba, Herr Ritter, Baba is an artist in the kitchen! Exquisite school of cooking! Works of art. Her whipped cream cake! After the eternal pub grub I've been eating—

RITTER: Indeed. Bohemian women all cook well. But their German is scandalous. Every day I get annoyed again. The young one will never learn it. And they've forgotten their mother tongue. They speak that gibberish even with each other. They're only half human after all, these Slavs.

CARL (*sarcastically*): The race of the future.

RITTER: May God protect me from the future! (*Goes back to Isolde's door to listen and returns.*) Did you—everything all right at home? Your mother and sister?

CARL: Are well. Already looking forward to seeing me when I go home for the semester break.

RITTER: They write to you often—your family?

CARL: Every day.

RITTER: And you?

CARL: Me, too. Recently a letter got lost in the mail. Mother telegraphed immediately.

RITTER (*smiling and shaking his head*): Women—coddled emotionally. (*Absentminded, since he keeps listening at*

21

Isolde's door.) So this summer you will travel together—to the mountains?

CARL: No. To the Netherlands. I am supposed to become
acquainted with the great art galleries.

RITTER: From here one could have such nice outings.
Two to three hours. Then you'd be right in the
middle—of the mountains.

CARL: If you ever wanted to—

RITTER: But Carl—as you can see—I can't leave home for
an hour without—do you think I can so much as go
to the throne in peace? I'd like to . . . with you—and
a few of your friends—

CARL (*shrugging his shoulders*): Oh, them! No, really: I
don't have any friends.

RITTER (*plays piano on his left hand, using the five fingers of his
right hand*): Carl! Carl! Surely, you must have found
some friends among the thousands of students—

CARL: No. None of them understand me.

RITTER (*raising his eyebrows*): Well!! (*Looking at the photograph of Beethoven.*) Poor Beethoven.

CARL: I am entirely mired in pessimism.

RITTER: And because you're a pessimist, you cut—

CARL: My classes.

RITTER: Well, I didn't think you cut out the pub—

CARL: Herr Ritter, I cut going there more often than I cut
class.

22

RITTER: Young man! Surely you're not—

CARL (*laughing*): Pulling your leg? (*Suddenly serious.*) I am an unhappy creature. I don't have it in me to be a real student.

RITTER: Oh, come now! Your father was one, after all. Quite a good one. And given the resemblance—let me look at you. That's just the way he looked. Down to the tiniest bits of mustache hair.

CARL: Take my word for it, I am not cut out to be a student. I can't stomach the drink, my smoking is so-so, and I enjoy the shouting and fighting even less.

RITTER: You know something? You were at home too long. In a small town, with your mother and sister. It leads to a kind of girlish oversensitivity . . .

CARL: I can't take anything lightly. Nothing at all can I take lightly. The rudeness of others—and their filthiness—

RITTER (*shaking his head*): Hm—as I remember, a certain Goethe once—one always has to adapt to the taste of one's age.

CARL: Then I am too old for my comrades.

RITTER: Or else too young. You don't even know how young you are. (*He takes up pacing again, his hands behind his back.*) I can't breathe a word to my mother that Isolde is worse.

CARL: You hear good things from her?

RITTER: Passable. An old woman—of course she's got complaints.

CARL: How long have you been here now?

RITTER: Almost six months. You arrived just about four weeks after us.

CARL: Don't you miss Vienna at all?

RITTER: Not Vienna. But my job. My job as conductor. And here, there have been anti-Wagnerian tendencies in the past few years. The intellectual climate is not—but if Isolde is better, I'd even live in America.

CARL: Do you think that would be so terrible?

RITTER: Oh! Their musical dilettantism! They produce music like shoes. People there don't have an inner ear. Intellectual types, all of them. Music needs feeling, imagination. But if the pure intellect begins to imagine—what will be the result? Caricatures.

CARL: But their inventions—they are—colossal.

RITTER (*again taking out his watch*): What do I want with their inventions. Eight o'clock. It's enough to drive one insane, this waiting. I really do have to have a telephone connection installed, directly to the clinic. Then we could do without the messengers and—

ANNA (*enters, visibly confused, through the hallway door*): Herr—Anton is arrived and he has brought with—

RITTER (*wants to go out the door*): The professor—

ANNA: No. Lady.

RITTER: What?

CARL (*simultaneously*): Phew!

ANNA: Lady says, she is doctor.

RITTER: Nonsense! (*To Carl.*) Do you understand this?

CARL: No-oh. Or else—what do I know—

RITTER: At any rate—ask the lady to come in.

ANNA (*exits*)

CARL: Of course, I've heard some gossip—Herr Gre-
gers—he's a medic—he said, maybe two weeks ago,
Berger had taken a woman as his assistant.

RITTER: But for him to send me someone like that—

ANNA (*opens the door and permits Sabine to enter*)

SABINE (*of medium height, slender but not thin. Narrow pale
face, but no unhealthy pallor. Small mouth, firmly
closed. Very bright, large, and calm eyes. She is wearing
a light-gray summer dress. Straight skirt, blouse with a
turned collar that leaves the neck uncovered. Broad black
silken belt without a bow. Black straw hat with a border
of openwork, trimmed with black tulle and black ribbon.
Her entire dress is simple and fashionable. Very good
gloves made of gray Danish leather. Sabine's voice is
clear and soft. Very economical movements. To Ritter,
who gives her an embarrassed bow, which she answers
with a light and casual nod of her head*): Herr Ritter?

CARL (*retreats discreetly to the desk and turns the leaves of a book lying there*)

RITTER: Yes—with whom do I have the—

SABINE: My name is Graef. I am an assistant in Professor Berger's clinic. I've been there for three weeks.

RITTER: The professor will not come?

SABINE: He had to leave town suddenly this morning. A serious illness in the family—

RITTER: And—(*he falters*).

SABINE: The—other assistants? Both gentlemen are engaged tonight. (*Without a trace of irony.*) A banquet. I have taken over duties for the night. And since your messenger said it was very urgent—

RITTER (*has composed himself somewhat*): Excuse my—my confusion.

SABINE (*always very straightforward, without any intention of irony*): Of course—it is justified—given the circumstances.

CARL (*who has half listened to the conversation, looks up in astonishment and begins to observe Sabine closely*)

RITTER: Please, if you will take a seat—

SABINE: Thank you. (*She sits down and unbuttons her gloves.*)

RITTER: Permit me to inform my daughter—she would perhaps be fright— too surprised—

SABINE: Please do.

RITTER (*goes to Isolde's door, knocks gently and enters on the tips of his toes. Short pause. Sabine takes off her hat. Straight dark hair, parted in the middle and collected in a bun in the back of her neck*)

CARL (*approaches her*): In all the excitement, Herr Ritter has neglected to introduce me. With your permission—(*bows*) my name is Curtius.

SABINE (*nods slightly and remains silent*)

CARL: You are related to the distinguished oculist Dr. Gräfe?

SABINE: No. My name is Graef. Without the final *e*.

CARL: Will you stay here long?

SABINE: I don't know yet. Originally, I had planned to go to Berlin.

CARL: Are you from the north?

SABINE: By birth. But I have been away for a long time.

CARL: You've been abroad?

SABINE: Yes. Most recently, in Paris.

CARL: Oh. Do the conditions here suit you, then?

SABINE (*calmly, but curtly*): The clinic is good. I am working. That is enough for me.

CARL (*feels that he has been awkward, bites his lips, and is silent. Pause*)

SABINE (*notices his embarrassment, somewhat more friendly*): You—are a student?

CARL: Yes. Of art history. Third semester.

SABINE: I assume you are related to Herr Ritter?

CARL: No. He was a good friend of my father's. And Isolde, when she was a child, spent a summer with us—

SABINE: Isolde—his daughter?

CARL: Yes.

SABINE: An only child—or— (*She pauses as if remembering something, laughs gently, and blushes.*)

CARL (*surprised*): Miss Graef . . . ?

SABINE (*frank and cordial, but not lively*): A moment ago I was annoyed because you asked me so many questions. I don't like to be interrogated in this manner. But now I did the same to you. Because it is part of the situation. Pardon me.

RITTER (*returns, leaving the door somewhat open, dim light shining through the door*): If you please . . .

SABINE (*rises, goes to the door, pauses for a moment*): If I could have a lamp for the examination—no shade—and not too tall—

RITTER: There is one like that in the room. I will light it immediately. (*He follows Sabine, who has gone ahead. Through the half-open door, one can see the light getting brighter. Ritter returns and closes the door behind him.*)

RITTER: Can you believe it!! Did she say anything—to you?

CARL: Yes.

RITTER: Did she talk nonsense?

CARL: Nah.

RITTER: What's your impression of her?

CARL: To judge by the snapshot—well, she isn't stupid.

RITTER: But a woman! How can such a petticoat have any sense? A thimbleful of sense—at the most.

CARL: She's strangely reticent for a woman who's been to a university. Her laughter isn't common. Not common at all. And I judge women by their laughter.

RITTER (*scratches his head*): Tricky situation.

CARL: I bet Isolde was floored?

RITTER: Not really. I said to her I'd take it upon myself to get rid of Miss—Miss—Miss Whatever-Her-Name-Is. "No. I want to try her. If she tells me to do something stupid, I won't do it."

CARL: Berger wouldn't take someone as his assistant who doesn't know the job. Any mistakes would be on his head. He'd be an *asinus quadratus*—

RITTER: Dear boy!! The Great Gentlemen—and what is more, the Great Gentlemen Doctors! Steal a little and you'll be hung, steal a lot and you'll be let go. One is completely at their mercy. Doctors and voice teachers—the same fraud.

CARL: Don't you want to go in? Please don't let me keep you—

RITTER: Not in the least. Isolde never permits me to be present during an examination. She has always talked with the doctors alone and—

SABINE (*half opens the door, talking back into the bedroom*): I'll be right back.

RITTER (*simultaneously to Carl*): You see! Already finished! Some examination.

SABINE (*comes in; her face doesn't show any change*): I will write a prescription. Please have it filled at once. Is the apothecary far from here?

RITTER: Right next door.

SABINE (*goes to the desk*): May I?

RITTER: Of course—but the candle . . .

SABINE: Will be enough. (*She has sat down, tears a prescription slip out of her notebook, writes quickly and with certainty.*)

RITTER (*runs to Isolde's door, speaking into the room in a hushed voice*): Bonni—how are you, my child?

ISOLDE'S VOICE (*weakly*): Thank you—well.

SABINE (*has heard, looks at the door for a second in astonishment, then lowers her head with a sad expression and quickly continues to write*)

RITTER: Carl is here—can he come see you later for a moment?

SABINE (*looking up*): Excuse me—Miss Isolde needs complete rest. She cannot receive anyone today. Please don't talk to her at the moment, either. It fatigues her.

RITTER (*cowed, creeps to Carl, who is standing near the hallway door*): Pretty soon I won't dare to do anything anymore. Whatever I do is wrong. I only want the best, after all. (*He rings the bell.*)

SABINE (*quickly checking the prescription, again puts the pen to paper*): For Miss Isolde—(*over her shoulder to Ritter*) Ritter—with two t's?

RITTER: Yes.

SABINE (*quickly finishes writing. Ritter and Carl speak in hushed voices*)

ANNA (*comes in. Ritter signals for her to wait*)

SABINE (*has risen and gives Ritter, who approaches her, the prescription*): Urgent. I indicated that on the prescription. Please be so kind as to call me when the medicine is here. (*She goes into Isolde's room.*)

RITTER (*gives the prescription to Anna*): Get a move on! Get a move on! Quickly!

ANNA (*exits*)

CARL (*pointing to the bedroom*): Please—excuse me—be so kind—and still, she orders one around—she's got energy.

RITTER: Female energy. Unartistic, primal. Not the energy that comes from rational thought. (*Goes to the serving table and pours a glass of wine.*) Here you go, Carl. (*Offers him the basket with pastries.*) Have some. Your stomach must be rumbling.

CARL: Thanks. (*Raises the glass toward the door.*) Get better! (*Drinks.*) None for you?

RITTER: I can't. By the way—she must have a lovely alto voice. Did you hear?

CARL: Her—sing? I don't think she knows any songs.

RITTER: I don't know—judging from sound of her speech— she's got something musical about her. A certain toneful piano—the kind that only works for alto voices.

CARL: She is terribly quiet. Hardly any movement at all. As if her limbs were glued together. I wouldn't want her as a dancing dummy.

RITTER: That's still better than a fluttering kind of disposition. If you're accustomed to the Viennese ragtags—

CARL: Are you going on again about the poor Austrians? After all, you yourself—

RITTER: Unfortunately. But I've cured myself of my birth. That isn't the main thing anymore.

CARL: Do you like the south Germans, then?

RITTER: Beer people.

CARL: What then? The north Germans?

RITTER: What? Those martial strutters?

CARL: Well, who, then?

RITTER: Nobody. I am a misanthrope. The world is too modern for my taste.

ANNA (*comes in, breathless, carrying a small bottle wrapped in green paper and the prescription in an envelope*): Is ready, medicine.

RITTER (*takes the bottle and envelope from her, knocks at Isolde's door and passes the bottle inside*)

CARL (*to Anna*): That fast?

ANNA: Apothecary knows me purty good. We eat much medicine. (*Exits.*)

RITTER (*comes to the front and takes the prescription out of the envelope*): Still, I've got to have a look.

CARL (*also looking at the prescription*): At least she doesn't have a scrawl, like most of them.

RITTER (*reads*): "Eserine sulf. 0.1 Aqu. Dest. 10.0. Four times daily one drop into the left eye—" (*Pauses.*) Eserine? What kind of a novelty is that? Isolde has never had this before. Atropine, cocaine, but eserine—she can't have got a completely new illness all of a sudden.

CARL (*also taken aback, shakes his head*): Maybe it was a slip of the pen?

SABINE (*comes out of the bedroom. She closes the door silently and carefully. In her left hand she is carrying the lamp, which Ritter politely takes from her and sets on the table*): You will permit me to remain for a while longer. Just a few moments. I would like to see the effects

33

of the eserine. And I have a few questions—if you have the time.

CARL (*quickly to Ritter*): I will go and render the garden unsafe. Imbibe a bit of moonshine—

RITTER (*nods to him. Carl exits over the stairs. Ritter offers Sabine a chair*): Mademoiselle— (*Sits down opposite her.*)

SABINE (*very simply*): Please—Miss Graef.

RITTER (*slightly inclining his head*): As you— (*Falling back into worry and agitation.*) And the eye? How long will it last? Is she in great pain? Is her condition dangerous? You will tell me the truth, won't you?

SABINE: — — It's serious.

RITTER (*leans back, places his forehead in his hands, very pale, but with a moving tranquillity*): — — A bad inflammation of the iris?

SABINE: No iritis.

RITTER: What then?

SABINE: An increase of intraocular pressure. Secondary glaucoma.

RITTER (*looking at her uncomprehendingly*): Forgive me— what is that?

SABINE: I wasn't able to conduct a thorough examination today. Given the intense irritation of the eye, I would have tortured the patient—and uselessly. The refractive media are very clouded.

RITTER: The cornea.

34

SABINE (*half smiling*): The cornea—correct. I think by to-morrow the pressure will—

RITTER (*interrupting with some relief*): So we can count upon an improvement, and soon?

SABINE: Certainly.

RITTER: And this attack won't have harmed her—

SABINE (*lifting her shoulders slightly*): That—perhaps a slight limitation of peripheral vision—but I hope— given the youthful elasticity of the vascular walls— You know that the eye has suffered in all its parts from the extended inflammation. Especially the synechia—I mean—

RITTER: Please, I know all about synechia. They're growths in the iris.

SABINE (*pulls out her notebook*): I had the patient relate the course of the illness to me as briefly as possible. Perhaps you have some corrections to make, based on your memory of it—

RITTER (*straightens somewhat and looks at Sabine with tense and thoughtful attention*)

SABINE (*reading from her notebook, with a professional de-meanor*): First symptoms in the left eye four years ago.

RITTER: Yes—on June 14—I was just on my way to the Musicians Association meeting—

SABINE (*continuing defensively, not permitting him to interrupt her*): —symptoms: slight decrease in vision. No pain, no visible change.

RITTER: Yes, there was—it—it looked a little dim—compared with the healthy eye. — Oh, she had such beautiful eyes.

SABINE: Six months later, intense and acute inflammation. Continuous and chronic irritation. Necessitates the daily use of atropine. Nevertheless intensified return of the inflammation. Resulting in a dimming of the cornea, numerous growths, and increasing loss of vision. The right eye—

RITTER: Not that the one eye wasn't enough!

SABINE: The right eye experienced a slight sympathetic inflammation two years ago. Benign, quick recovery. Hardly any loss of vision.

RITTER: None at all, none at all. Isolde says she could read even the tiniest script in the doctors' testing books, with her right eye.

SABINE (*astonished*): Brilliant script? But she said— (*Reconsidering, conceding.*) A precise examination will— at the moment, that is beside the point. You have consulted many doctors—

RITTER: Every authority in Vienna. It was no use.

SABINE (*quietly*): That is in the nature of the disease. And you used many different medications.

RITTER (*sighing*): That, too. A veritable torment. And on
top of it all, old Stellwag was so rough—

SABINE: Finally, the most extreme remedy: mercury injections under the skin. (*Looking up from her notebook.*) Do you have a prescription for that?

RITTER: No. The doctor didn't want to give us one. He always brought the mercury along with him. I don't
know why.

SABINE (*looking at him with astonishment and suspicion*):
You don't know why? You don't have to keep the
secret from me. I know why.

RITTER (*half surprised, half intimidated*): I really don't
know why.

SABINE (*bites her lip and raises her eyebrows somewhat. Continuing, more coldly than before*): Do you remember
whether Isolde really received twenty-two injections one after the other? That is an unusual number. There is no error here?

RITTER (*gets up hastily and walks to the desk*): No. No. That's
it exactly. I can look it up in my diary— (*Takes a
medium-sized black bound book out of the middle drawer
of the desk, turns its leaves for a moment.*) Where do I
have—where is it—here: October 4—

SABINE: Of last year?

RITTER: Last year. (*Reads.*) "Today was an exceedingly important day, the day on which Isolde received her

final injection, number 22. As a reward for her patience—" (*Stops.*) Well then.

SABINE: And that was also when the greatest improvement occurred?

RITTER: In her vision—in the left eye. She could read newspaper titles again: *New Free Press.*

SABINE: You moved here on account of your daughter?

RITTER: Yes. Vienna is altogether the wrong climate for people suffering from eye disease. That perpetual wind and chalk dust. There were also social and familial circumstances we wanted to get away from. And above all, we were attracted by Professor Berger's reputation.

SABINE: Why didn't you check your daughter into the clinic?

RITTER (*in a haughty and somewhat contemptuous tone of voice*): No-oh. To abandon my child to the arbitrary moods of these nurses. That would go against my principles. I would have died with worry. My child . . . ! The professor advocated discontinuing all medications.

SABINE: After they had all failed. And his prognosis?

RITTER: Is relatively favorable. (*Half correcting himself.*) Well, if you can call it favorable, given the circumstances. The inflammation will gradually recede and her vision will gradually improve. It can't get back to normal, but!! We are content with so little. Peace! Rest! After four years! Finally!

SABINE (*observantly*): People around her also suffer—

RITTER: Me? What do I matter? But she should still get something out of life. I'm finished with that circus show. But my child—to see such a young life perish before your eyes . . . it's hard.

SABINE: What did they tell you was the principal cause of the disease?

RITTER: This and that. Everyone had a different theory. The chills, anemia, tuberculosis of the eye—

SABINE: Your daughter never had rheumatism in the joints?

RITTER: Not a hint.

SABINE: And nobody ever told you—why the—specific remedy—mercury—was used with such intensity?

RITTER: I thought—mercury is a general remedy for all eye diseases.

SABINE: Certainly. But in your daughter's case, it was used to such a degree—an iritis is usually only treated in this manner if it is the result of a general disease.

RITTER: Isolde has always been as healthy as a horse.

SABINE: Has your daughter ever been examined by a gynecologist?

RITTER: Yes. In Vienna.

SABINE: At whose suggestion?

RITTER: The young doctor—Professor Fuchs. The young ones are always so coarse.

SABINE: And the result? Do you know anything about that?

RITTER (*takes his diary up again and turns its leaves*): Here is the letter—

SABINE: May I? (*Takes it, reading in a low voice.*) "Dear colleague, my examination of Miss Ritter has yielded only a negative result—her eye condition cannot be explained in this manner"—etc., etc. Where did you get this letter?

RITTER: Fuchs said it was an important reference and I should keep it.

SABINE: And you did not find any of this dubious?

RITTER (*his eyes round*): No.

SABINE (*impulsively*): That is hardly cred— (*Stops. A short, thoughtful pause.*) Your eyes are healthy? (*During the following sentences she takes a leather case out of her bag, opens it, retrieves an eye mirror and a magnifying glass, cleans both with a piece of chamois.*)

RITTER: Yes, my vision is good. Only very fine notes are a bit difficult for me now—and particularly the French scores, they're so poorly printed. After I conducted the *Damnation*, my eyes burned like fire.

SABINE: Please sit down opposite me—like this—and pull up close—all the way—

RITTER (*pulls toward her until his knees are touching hers. Both of them are sitting sideways in front of the table. Sabine rises to turn the overhead light down completely, so that the standing lamp remains the only light source. After she has carefully wiped her fingers with her handkerchief, she takes up the magnifying glass*)

SABINE: Please look at me. (*After she has gazed first at one, then at the other eye for a moment without touching them, she exposes both to the light that passes through the magnifying glass, held sideways. She does all this quickly and confidently.*) Is the light hurting your eyes?

RITTER: It's a bit—uncomfortable.

SABINE (*lowers the magnifying glass*): You can rest your eyes now for a moment.

RITTER: Please—it's not that bad.

SABINE (*adjusts the lamp so that it stands partly behind Ritter, takes an eye mirror into her right hand, while she carefully pulls apart the lids of one eye*): With your permission—your lids are a bit heavy—please look up—down—to your right—to your left—please look at my nose—

RITTER (*spontaneously begins to laugh*)

SABINE (*lowers the eye mirror*)

RITTER (*highly embarrassed*): Oh, pardon me.

SABINE (*also somewhat amused, pleasantly*): I cannot spare you the necessity of looking at my nose.

RITTER (*forces himself to be serious*): Oh, with pleasure.

SABINE: Just for a second. (*Raises the eye mirror again, examines the other eye in the same manner.*) Up—down—right—left—at the middle . . . Thank you. (*Replaces the instruments in the case and turns on the overhead light.*) Your eyes are normal. I have a few more questions. Please answer me as succinctly as possible.

RITTER: Impartially and concisely.

SABINE: And honestly.

RITTER (*moves back slightly. Not offended but with reticent earnestness*): I will.

SABINE (*takes notes of Ritter's subsequent answers in her notebook. She uses shorthand, which is indicated by the movements of her hand*): Do you know whether there were other serious eye diseases in your family or in your wife's family?

RITTER: Not in my family. My father was somewhat shortsighted . . .

SABINE: Did he work in a profession that is damaging to eyesight?

RITTER: No. He was a piano builder and the owner of the Ritter Piano Factory in Vienna. And my mother doesn't need eyeglasses to this day. My wife's family—a veritable race of pirates. Indestructible, all of them.

SABINE: So there were no cases of lung or heart disease?

RITTER: I lost my wife—should I slow down a bit—because you're taking notes?

SABINE: No thank you. I write shorthand. Your wife died of—

RITTER: Five years ago, of acute pneumonia.

SABINE: Were her lungs affected before this?

RITTER: No. She caught a cold at a ball—very severe—and eight days later— (*He falls silent and looks at the floor.*)

SABINE: You were married at the age of—

RITTER (*reflecting*): Now, I really don't remember—at twenty-seven or twenty-eight—I think at twenty-seven—the year the *Meistersinger* was performed for the first time—

SABINE: Your wife was—

RITTER: Twenty years old.

SABINE: And your daughter was born—

RITTER: A year and a half later.

SABINE: No miscarriage before?

RITTER (*blushing*): No.

SABINE: Your wife was well—nothing unusual occurred during pregnancy?

RITTER (*blushing harder, increasingly embarrassed*): Yes—I mean, no.

SABINE: The birth?

RITTER: Was difficult.

SABINE: With forceps?

RITTER: No.

SABINE: Your wife nursed the child herself?

RITTER: No. That wasn't the custom in Vienna. We had a wet nurse. A Slovak woman.

SABINE: Was she healthy?

RITTER: Our family physician said she was—very.

SABINE: Did the child suffer from sore corners of the mouth during the first years of life? Rashes? Ulcers about the gums?

RITTER: I can't say. Back then, I was almost constantly on concert tour, and my wife accompanied me.

SABINE: The child was left with the servants?

RITTER: What are you thinking! With my parents.

SABINE: There were no further children?

RITTER: No. My wife was very relieved.

SABINE: When did puberty set in with your daughter?

RITTER (*blushing furiously*): I think—at—at age fourteen.

SABINE: Was she anemic—bloodless?

RITTER: Never ever.

SABINE: Did she strain her eyes? Needlework—in the evenings?

RITTER: Not that either. She did a lot of drawing, later she took up painting—porcelain and watercolors—eminently talented. (*Points at the picture.*) Her work.

SABINE (*looks up*): A self-portrait? In a ballgown? Did she visit many balls and social gatherings?

44

RITTER: My wife introduced her into society relatively early. It was so pretty. They looked like sisters.

SABINE: One moment. (*Quickly reads through her notes, murmuring.*) Nothing, nothing at all. Only— (*Again looks at Ritter piercingly.*) You have never had a serious physical ailment?

RITTER: No.

SABINE (*looking at her notebook*): You were married at—at age twenty-seven. I assume that previous to this you lived like young people do—

RITTER (*blushes dark red, interrupts her vehemently*): Please, Mademoiselle. I was engaged to my wife for five years.

SABINE: Such an extended period of engagement usually does not present an obstacle.

RITTER (*jumps up*): Listen, you—you've got some nice opinions.

SABINE: I don't have any opinions at all. Just experience.

RITTER (*vehemently, but trying to control himself*): You're supposed to confine your questions to the field of medicine. But there are things that are supposed to be treated as secrets.

SABINE: There are also things that have to be stripped of their aura and their secretiveness. That is what makes them dangerous.

RITTER: I don't even see why this should be a subject of conversation between us. Useless! (*Stops before her.*) Aren't you embarrassed at all?

SABINE: You either don't understand me or you don't want to understand me.

RITTER (*helplessly clapping his hands together*): For God's sake! I don't understand you.

SABINE: You are to tell me whether the possibility of a specific hereditary contamination, from the paternal side, is out of the question.

RITTER: And you really think I know what a specific hereditary contamination is?

SABINE (*is silent for a moment, then as calmly as everything she has said before*): Syphilis.

RITTER (*his hands in his pants pockets, still looking at her without comprehending. He repeats tonelessly*): Syphilis— (*Slowly remembering the sound of the word.*) What?? (*Jumps up, both hands at his forehead, incensed.*) Are you insane? (*Breaking into furious laughter.*) Perhaps you also think me capable of stealing silver spoons.

SABINE (*unperturbed*): So it is not?

RITTER: Ridiculous! Simply ridiculous! And you ought to have known that a cultured person—

SABINE (*smiling disdainfully*): Right! Those cultured people—

RITTER: Yes, and the moral footing—

SABINE (*her face has turned dark and serious*): The weakest point in the physical and mental organism is the moral footing. Every physician knows that.

RITTER: Then if I were you, I would assume I'm lying.

SABINE (*looks at him*): Lie—and maybe make your child blind, you couldn't do that. Your ignorance of the disease misled me. That's why I had to ask. You answered—I believe you. — I will look in on her once more. (*Goes into the bedroom.*)

RITTER (*runs his fingers through his hair, runs to the balcony door, throws it wide open, and calls out*): Carl!

CARL (*enters after a few moments*): Did she talk a lot more nonsense—

RITTER (*still at the height of fury*): That's what you get! That's what you get when womenfolk study medicine! I am a decent person. And then such a dirty trick! I ask you, Carl, look at me. What do I look like? Do I look like a—like—it is incredible. And there she stands, this woman—and she isn't even old—and she uses a language—well! The devil take all this modern crap!

CARL: Modern crap, that's a good one.

RITTER (*wipes the sweat off his forehead with his handkerchief*): Enough to make one's blood boil. I sweated blood. Do you think that even one of the twenty doctors we had the pleasure of consulting ever dared to ask the kinds of questions that she asked?

CARL: Maybe it would have been better if they *had* asked.

RITTER: Not at all. That is so typical of women. The need for something extraordinary, something extra special—that excites their little brains—but nary a word of compassion for my child—

SABINE (*returns, leaves the door relatively wide open*): She's better.

RITTER (*his face lightens up, he half emits a joyful sound*): Ah—less pain.

SABINE: She will be able to sleep. Without morphine. If she still wishes to eat something, only a cup of beef broth.

RITTER: Bouillon—

SABINE: Yes. She is not allowed to chew anything. The chewing motion could irritate the eye. If she's thirsty, give her a little wine mixed with water. I don't think there'll be intense pain during the night. If there is—give her one drop of eserine—just one.

RITTER (*uncertainly*): And tomorrow morning?

SABINE: I will send you the first assistant, Doctor Horn.

RITTER (*is silent for a moment while Sabine puts on her hat*): You wouldn't have the kindness—

SABINE: No. (*The bell in Isolde's room is rung vigorously.*)

RITTER (*runs inside. One can hear him speaking half audibly with Isolde*)

CARL: Mademoiselle has concluded that the ailment is very serious?

SABINE: — It is a serious illness.

CARL: Isolde is greatly to be pitied.

SABINE: And her father even more.

RITTER (*returns, embarrassed*): I am supposed to ask you— my daughter requests—that you return tomorrow.

SABINE: I regret—

RITTER (*takes both her hands and looks at her half pleadingly, half accusingly*): But I beg you—

SABINE (*defeated*): — Then tomorrow—at eight o'clock. (*She removes her hands from his and hastily pulls her gloves on.*)

RITTER: If you will be patient for a moment—I'll call for a carriage immediately.

SABINE: No, thank you. I don't need a carriage. I prefer to walk. I want to walk.

RITTER: But you can't, this late at night—

SABINE: Yes, I can.

CARL: It goes without saying—

SABINE: Please don't trouble yourself.

CARL: I am walking the same way.

RITTER: Yes, do, Carl. Take care of Miss Graef. And poor boy, you didn't even get anything to eat.

CARL: I'll stop at the sausage stand.

SABINE: Good night, Herr Ritter.

CARL (*shaking his hands*): Yes—good night. I'll look in tomorrow morning.

RITTER (*accompanies them to the door, returns immediately, followed by Anna*): I won't eat anything now—no. Clear the table. (*Goes to Isolde's room, pushing back the door at the right and the left.*) I'll open up, Bonni. So you'll get some air. (*The view opens up into a small room. The bed against the back wall, lengthwise. Rococo curtains. Bedside table with medicine bottles and a water glass. A wardrobe with a mirror door, washstand with a mirror. On the elegant dressing table draped with lace, a night lamp burns under a green glass shade. All pieces of furniture are lacquered in white with light-blue stripes. Isolde deep in her pillows, barely visible. Ritter kneels at the bed and kisses her hands, which are hanging down.*)

RITTER: How are you?

ISOLDE (*in a soft but labored voice*): Thank you—well — —
how do you like her?

RITTER: Well . . . !

ISOLDE: . . . Her hands are so soft.

RITTER: Don't talk, don't talk—it will fatigue you.

ISOLDE: — Papa!

RITTER: What, my child?

ISOLDE: Do you love me?

RITTER: Come now!

ISOLDE: I mean—so terribly much—more than anything else—only me?

RITTER: Yes yes!!!

ISOLDE: More than Grandmama?

RITTER: Yes.

ISOLDE (*turns on her other side, satisfied*): I want to sleep.

RITTER (*gets up, kisses her hands again*): Good night. (*Tiptoes into the living room; to Anna who has just finished clearing the table.*) Sleeping. Shh. (*Pours himself a glass of wine and hastily drinks it. Goes to the veranda door and throws the bolt.*)

ANNA (*exits with her tray*): Good night, Herr—

RITTER (*signals her hastily and angrily*): Shhh!!! (*Sits down on a chair, takes off his boots and places them in front of the door. Goes into his bedroom and comes out after a few seconds, now in shirtsleeves, with a pillow and blanket. He clumsily makes his bed on the sofa. Unbuttoning his suspenders, he again cautiously glances at Isolde. Walking to the front of the stage, he stops in front of the chair in which Sabine sat down. Sits down on the sofa, puts his head into his hands, quietly to himself, his eyes always on Sabine's chair.*) Well . . .

ACT II

*Bright summer afternoon. The table has been moved to the
middle of the stage, away from the sofa and set for afternoon coffee for four persons. Exquisite china, silver baskets
with sweets and fruit, a crystal vase with summer flowers.*

ANNA (*arranges plates, small knives and spoons on the serving
    table*)

ISOLDE (*wearing her eyeglasses, a white dress with a light-blue
    sash, rosebuds in her belt. She is lying comfortably on the
    sofa and wagging a patent leather shoe, which is half off
    her foot, on the tip of her toe. Beside her, a poorly dressed
    girl of nine years, her hair drawn away from her face and
    braided into a stiff ponytail in the back*)

ISOLDE (*somewhat impatiently*): No, darling, not today. Your
    mama was supposed to come read tomorrow. Tell
    her tomorrow afternoon at three o'clock—adieu.

CHILD (*shyly handing over an envelope*): Mama said with
    your permission—

ISOLDE (*accepting it*): Ah—have we already had ten hours—I'll give her the money tomorrow—there's no hurry—I really don't have time today— (*Puts the envelope in her bag while staring at the child.*) Why don't you wear your hair down? That braid in the back is ugly—I will give you a ribbon. Tomorrow. Tell your mama to remind me. Adieu (*holds out her hand to the child*). There—you may kiss my hand—it's not a bad thing for little girls to learn manners.

CHILD (*clumsily kisses her hand*)

ISOLDE: You may go through the garden—the door is open.

CHILD (*curtseys and turns to leave*)

ISOLDE (*rising*): Wait a minute—I have something— (*Has gone to the table, selected a big piece of cake and gives it to the child.*) There, my love. Take a big bite. Is it good? How is your piano playing these days? I have to tell Papa to test you soon. There, chicken. Adieu. (*The child exits through the veranda.*)

ANNA (*comes to the table and puts a water glass in front of each place setting*): Mademoiselle has such good heart.

ISOLDE: One should always do good to the poor—and I can't stand it, a child like that looking at the cake. And we have so much of it. Is the whipped cream on ice—is it stiff?

ANNA: Hard as a rock.

ISOLDE: Tell Baba to brew the coffee slowly, very slowly. It has to be exquisitely good. I don't want to be embarrassed when Miss Graef is with us for the first time. One and a half spoons per cup. And above all, don't forget—boiled cream and cold. The cold in the silver jug. If there's any whipped cream left over, you may eat it.

ANNA (*exits through the front room*)

ISOLDE (*goes around the table, scrutinizing it once more, wipes the inside of a cup with the little finger of her right hand to see if there is dust in it. She holds a water glass up to the light, replaces it quickly on the table and passes her hand over her eyes*): Ouch! (*Takes several candies from one of the bowls and walks around the room, eating and humming to herself.*) "Yes, such a man can be a charmer, such a charmer . . ." (*Opens up the piano, tries to play the melody with one finger, misses the right key, and angrily runs her thumb over two octaves. Bored, throws herself into the desk chair, yawning.*) Bo-oring— dreadfully boring. (*Pulls a small mirror out of her bag and makes faces at herself.*) Ooo— Aaa. (*Rhythmically beating both hands on her knees.*) Tin, ten, tan, ton, tun . . . (*Looks at the table, her glance arrested, with interest, by the bouquet of flowers. She moves her head in intense observation, quickly opens a desk drawer and takes out a sketchbook. Runs to the table, arranges the flowers, care-*

fully checks at the veranda door whether anyone is coming, seats herself with her back to the veranda, takes off her glasses, and eagerly begins to draw. Occasionally, she wipes her left eye with her handkerchief.)

CARL *(comes in over the veranda, looks at Isolde, astounded, rushes to her, and tears the book out of her hand)*: Bonni—you monster!

ISOLDE *(jumps up with a cry and drops her pencil)*

CARL *(agitated)*: You deserve to be spanked!

ISOLDE *(laughing, reassured)*: Pray contain your wrath, Don Carlos. *(Lamenting.)* A pen, a pen, my kingdom for a pen!

CARL *(still agitated)*: You are a first-rate brute! Without your glasses! And drawing! Put your glasses on at once!

ISOLDE *(puts her glasses on, relaxed, trilling)*: "Slowly forward, slowly forward, and the Austrian men in arms—" *(Again in a lamenting tone.)* My pen—ah, but where is my pen? Under the table— *(Attempting to stoop.)*

CARL *(holds her back)*: Don't you dare stoop and let the blood rush into your head— I'll get it— *(Awkwardly kneels down and looks for the pencil under the table.)*

ISOLDE *(laughing)*: He kneels! Fat Carl kneels! Carl, your pants are about to split—oh, what a looker, what a looker! *(She is doubling up with laughter.)* Now I know what to write in your autograph album. I will make a drawing of you, just as you are lying there, and I'll sign it: "Live life happy, as you please, fat little rat in a mound of cheese."

CARL (*has found the pencil. Isolde pulls at one of his arms with both hands as he is getting up*)

ISOLDE: Ooofff! Get up, fat rat in the cheese! I'll write it in your album.

CARL: Album, schmalbum. (*Gives her the pencil.*) There. And the drawing must stop. Now that you're finally better, you have to do everything you can to get sick again? Right? And then you'll be down in the dumps again—

ISOLDE (*mocking, coquettish*): On my little rump—

CARL: And we'll be standing by tearing our hair out.

ISOLDE (*as previously*): My golden tresses— (*Humming the melody.*) Little brother, brother of mine, must you really rage and pine—

CARL: When will you stop your incessant singsong—

ISOLDE: Surely I will be permitted to express my musical spirit. No, but seriously. You are a silly boy and drawing won't hurt me. Just for a second—

CARL: Even half a second is too much. The worry you have caused me already!

ISOLDE: Whew! Look at him! The man reduced to a skeleton with worry! (*Tapping his stomach.*) Except for

56

his tummy. That grows and thrives like the lilies of the field. A lily-white tummy.

CARL (*blushes, goes to the desk where he puts down the sketchbook*): A fool, that's what you are. A selfish fool.

ISOLDE (*follows him, half mocking, half cajoling*): Little Carl, good fat little King Carl—of Iceland—you've always been the King of Iceland—

CARL (*grumbling crossly*): Rrrrr—

ISOLDE: Don't you grumble into your six beard hairs— they have grown by an entire millimeter—later, you'll get fed some good things—a real Viennese cream tart—simply delicious, to die for—I can already see you lying across your plate—and shoveling it in—mmmm—both cheeks full—and then he makes these fish eyes, he's that greedy—

CARL: Isolde—you'd better quit the teasing now—

ISOLDE (*thumbs her nose at him*): Losers quit.

CARL: You won't rest until you've got your spanking—

ISOLDE (*offers her face up to him*): Please don't hold back. A slap in the face—or—(*very coquettish*) a kiss?

CARL (*makes a vehement movement, as if to embrace her, then pauses, overcome with shyness, and turns away, anguished and blushing furiously*)

ISOLDE (*half angry, half amused, stamping her foot lightly*): God, are you stupid!

CARL (*has composed himself*): You—don't be so direct.

ISOLDE (*pouting, meanwhile walking about and teasing the ends of her braids*): When a pretty girl makes advances like this . . .

CARL (*in mock surprise*): You're supposed to be pretty—you?

ISOLDE: Don't pretend! You like me better than the whole big wide world.

CARL (*exaggeratedly*): You've got fleas in the head. I don't care what you think.

ISOLDE: And your poems? Hee-hee! (*Reciting.*) "In moonlight in the still spring night your countenance appears to me. My sleep is gone, my heart awakes and turns in fervent prayer to thee." (*In a regular voice.*) "In fervent prayer to thee." Pretty. Very pretty. Haven't I read that before somewhere? How funny that feels! I the heroine of a poem!

CARL: But Isolde, you're making a fool of yourself. They're not addressed to you, my poems!

ISOLDE: No? To whom then? Your hand as a sign that you are telling the truth.

CARL (*thinks for a moment, laughs, and gives her his hand*): To—Glaucopis.

ISOLDE (*very disappointed*): Glaucopis? Who on earth is that? What a silly name. How silly, Copis. How common.

CARL: Yes—that common Pallas Athena!

ISOLDE: Oh, come off it. Athena. She's probably a waitress somewhere.

CARL (*sits down comfortably at the table and sneaks a few candies*): Now you can squirm all you want, you curious Gretel. It'll be a long time before you'll get it.

ISOLDE (*throws herself moodily upon the sofa. With a long yawn from behind her hand*): Ohhhh.

CARL: What a jaw-cracker!

ISOLDE: Stop your gibberish. You are so boring—I could die.

CARL: How many times you've already died today . . .

ISOLDE: Have you heard nothing about her?

CARL: About whom?

ISOLDE: About that Graef woman! Of course!

CARL: Why of course? I'm not a spy.

ISOLDE: Don't be so condescending. Spy! What do you know about her? I'll even give you the Dieffenbach for a watch fob. Quickly, quickly, quickly!

CARL (*twiddling his thumbs*): Quickly but slow down.

ISOLDE: I wonder where she studied medicine?

CARL: In Zurich, of course! Where else. Womenfolk can't go to our universities.

ISOLDE: Womenfolk! How you're imitating Papa!

CARL: She also got her doctorate in Zurich. Summa cum laude.

ISOLDE: Does that mean she did well?

CARL: With highest honors — — Are you girls stupid!

ISOLDE: Latin snob! I bet the Graef woman is every bit as smart as you.

CARL: A clever scamp.

ISOLDE: I just don't understand how she can wear the same dress every day. The same one, always. One gets sick of looking at it.

CARL: She's also always wearing the same behavior.

ISOLDE: Strange! But she doesn't talk drivel. I know what kinds of doctors I had in the past—first off, they tell you their life stories. She doesn't say anything about herself directly. And when she touches you—those silken hands. That's what I liked so much about her, that first night. By the way, when she doesn't talk medicine—socially, she's as shy as a teenager.

CARL: She doesn't know anything at all about art. I thought to test her a little—about Italian paintings. An ignoramus. Do you think she's ever even set foot in the Munich Museum of Art? I don't think she knows a Phidias from a baker's boy.

ISOLDE: No culture at all.

ANNA (*half opens the bedroom door, holding out a few small bottles filled with a red liquid*): Mademoiselle—is that to throw away?

ISOLDE (*hastily jumps up and runs to the door*): What are you thinking? That's to be saved.

ANNA: But there is new bottle now.

ISOLDE: Save it!! Give me the flask on top of the toilet table.

ANNA (*disappears*)

CARL (*pointing at the two bottles, which Isolde is holding in her hands*): And what kind of delicacy is this?

ISOLDE (*with a funny kind of pride*): Poison. Eserine. But it's no use anymore. It's too old. It's already turned bright red. It turns red, it does, when it gets old. Ruby red, see?

CARL (*disgusted*): A nice ruby, what with the death's head on it and everything! Phew! Throw it away!

ISOLDE: Yes sir. I will follow your orders immediately.

ANNA (*gives Isolde a sealed flask through the door. The flask is already one-third full of red liquid*)

ISOLDE (*puts it on the desk and carefully empties the two little bottles into it*): Red poison. It's like straight from a tragedy. Before, the flask contained White Iris. Doesn't that give rise to psychological reflections, Carl?

CARL: Philosophical reflections.

ISOLDE: Oh, come now, that's all *toute même chose*. There, and now I'll glue—now I'll glue—a label on the vial—but what kind of motto will I write on it—something old—something medieval—I simply adore the Middle Ages.

CARL: But you, you are more rococo style—Venetian filigree.

ISOLDE: Aren't I now? That waist! And the Graef woman?

CARL: Pure Gothic—pointed arch.

ISOLDE (*while taking a label from a little box and dipping the pen into the ink*): And you?

CARL: Baroque—wig.

ISOLDE: Dense wig! Now I know. The motto. From *Tristan and Isolde*. "For deepest pain, for highest woe she gave the draught of death." The draught of death. It sounds so nice and scary, and I like scary things.

CARL: Where, by the way, is your fortunate progenitor?

ISOLDE (*pointing to Ritter's room with her pen, over her shoulder*): In there—I think. Don't disturb me, otherwise the ink will run.

CARL (*takes a piece of cake*): If you think you can invite me for afternoon coffee and then I'll wait till midnight—

ISOLDE (*writing*): "She—gave—" The Graef woman isn't coming till five. Time already?

CARL: No. A quarter of.

ISOLDE: "Draught of death." (*Dries what she has written with blotting paper and glues the label onto the bottle. Seeing that Carl is eating.*) One for me, too.

CARL (*offers her a bite*): Well, well. You're not quite ready for death yet.

ISOLDE (*calling*): Anna! — Right, death. As if I'd do you that favor, just so you can have all the cake to yourself.

ANNA (*comes out of the bedroom*)

ISOLDE (*hands her the two empty bottles*): Throw those away. And this one (*handing her the flask*) you'll put into the red plush case, the square one. The one that has the lavender salt in it.

ANNA (*exits*)

CARL: Poison and lavender salt—your ideas are inexhaustible.

RITTER (*comes through the hallway door, an open letter in his hand*): Ah! Don Carlos! *Salem aleikum.* Good day . . . you all right?

CARL: Thank you—so-so.

RITTER: What do you say to our child? How she looks? Those cheeks!

CARL: Indeed. Rubenesque baby cheeks—almost.

RITTER: Thank God, thank God! Well, that Graef woman! A capable woman. Strange bird! But really very clever. Really! (*Points at the letter in his hand.*) A letter, Bonni, from Grandmama. Overjoyed, of course, to hear you're better. Asking if we didn't want to come home—before the winter?

ISOLDE: Not for all the silk in Venice.

RITTER: Poor old mummy. I'm sorry for her. She misses us so much. And on top of that—to be almost seventy—and to be separated from us and all alone—

ISOLDE (*nervously fidgeting with her handkerchief*): I don't want to, I don't want to. (*Has thrown the envelope out of her pocket with the handkerchief. Carl picks it up and gives it to her.*) Papa, give me money. To pay for the reading. And I also need a few other things. I need a lot of money.

RITTER: A lot of my money! You're wheedling it out of me again.

ISOLDE: Wheedling it out—look how he's putting on airs!

RITTER: Bonni, you shouldn't refer to your papa as "he."

ISOLDE: You're surely not a she! He doesn't know anything about money, Carl, he, he, he.

RITTER: I did a nice job bringing her up! A splendid specimen! I'll write a few lines to Grandmama. Don't you want to add a few—

ISOLDE: I cannot write, my eyes—

RITTER: Just hugs and kisses—

ISOLDE (*stubbornly*): No, Papa, all that white paper, it'll blind me—no, no. That may harm me.

RITTER (*going toward his room*): Then don't.

ISOLDE: Won't you put on your black jacket?

RITTER: Of course. I have to look my best.

ISOLDE: And put on a different tie. The one you're wearing has seen better days.

RITTER: All right, that too. How a man is tormented! (*Off into his room.*)

CARL: You and your excuses! Why didn't you do him the favor?

ISOLDE (*purses her lips, sways, half dancing, from one foot to the other*): If I don't want to, I don't want to.

CARL: It seems to me that you don't like your grandmother.

ISOLDE: Oh—so-so. I don't get along with her.

CARL: A modern grandchild, straight from the *New Free Press*.

ISOLDE: Grandmama is too smart for my taste. I don't like people around me who have more brains than I do.

CARL: Thanks.

ISOLDE: You're welcome. Grandmama is a good person. Certainly. But Papa is everything to her. My Heinrich, my son, my Heinrich—nonstop, like a barrel organ. I am no more than the side dish. So I bugged Papa until we finally left.

CARL: Hard to believe that he gave up his brilliant conducting career so easily.

ISOLDE: It was not easy for him. Not at all.

CARL: He really lives only for you.

ISOLDE: Right. That's the way it should be.

CARL (*looking through the glass door of the veranda*): Ah—here she comes.

ISOLDE (*joining him*): Ah ha—that gray medicine bottle. (*Waves to Sabine.*) *Bon jour, bon jour*— (*In a low voice to Carl.*) My God, she is so utterly not pretty—she doesn't want to be pretty—or she doesn't think of wanting to be pretty—would you please ring for the servant girl to bring the coffee—

CARL (*rings*)

ISOLDE (*taking a few steps toward Sabine. Vivacious and with unintentional exaggeration*): How kind, how nice, how sweet of you, I am oh so delighted—

SABINE (*enters. She is dressed as she was in act 1, her color heightened from walking quickly*): Good afternoon, Miss. Why are you looking into the sun? You shouldn't. (*She nods slightly in response to Carl's bow and takes off her gloves.*)

CARL: The stories I could tell you of what Isolde shouldn't—

ISOLDE: Old chatterbox! Go and get Papa.

CARL (*knocks on Ritter's door and enters*)

SABINE: Let me take a quick look.

ISOLDE (*takes off her glasses*)

SABINE (*after she has looked into Isolde's eyes with a quick and discerning glance*): Now close them and look down (*she carefully touches first one, then the other eye, using the index and middle finger of both hands*). Good. Very good. The pressure is normal. You can put your glasses back on. (*Taking off her hat, which Isolde places on the piano with her gloves.*) The injection point is very small. You are not experiencing any pain?

ANNA (*has entered with a large tray, places it on the serving table, pours coffee into the cups, and places the coffeepots on the table*)

ISOLDE: Not really. It's just—I feel that I have an eye.

RITTER (*in his black jacket, Carl behind him. He shakes Sabine's hand warmly*): It's so nice that you have finally come to visit.

SABINE (*somewhat flustered*): Oh, please—it is I who must thank you for— (*Falls silent.*)

ISOLDE (*at the table*): The coffee is getting cold—please sit down—Fräulein von Graef here, and you, Papa, next to her—and Carl next to me. There we go. Everyone has to help himself, nobody will be pressed to eat, that's old-fashioned.

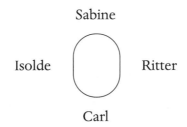

Sabine

Isolde   Ritter

Carl

RITTER (*sits down, takes a little coffee on a spoon, and lets it run back into his cup*): The color is good. (*Leans forward over his coffee cup to sniff it.*)

ISOLDE: Papa—don't stick your nose in it—behave yourself! (*To Sabine, apologetically.*) Coffee is Papa's passion. When it comes to coffee, he loses all self-control.

CARL (*chewing constantly and quickly, both cheeks full*): Toss me the sugar, please.

ISOLDE (*notices that Sabine is looking self-consciously at her cup*): Is it too strong for you?

SABINE (*still a little shy*): Yes—I—I'm not accustomed to coffee.

RITTER: You don't mean you don't drink any?

SABINE: I don't.

ISOLDE (*laughs*): Now you've ruined your chances with Papa.

RITTER: How can a proper person not drink coffee! And coffee like this—not the coffeehouse swill!

ISOLDE: Papa!! Don't be undiplomatic!

RITTER: What do you drink, then?

SABINE: Milk.

RITTER (*makes a face*): Yech! Thin brew—and causes heartburn, to boot.

ISOLDE: Why don't you try it—I'll give you lots of cream—and sugar—two lumps? Three?

SABINE: None, please.

ISOLDE: But Miss Graef, how can you make life so hard for yourself!

SABINE: I— (*Lapses into an embarrassed silence.*)

ISOLDE: Why don't you take any sugar?

SABINE: Years ago, I had to break the habit, and now I can't get used to it again.

ISOLDE: Why did you have to do that?

RITTER (*somewhat annoyed at her inquisitiveness*): Don't be so curious! Why? Because!

SABINE (*simply*): Oh—that is no secret. I was— (*She stumbles over the word and tries to find an alternative.*) I couldn't make ends— (*With sudden determination.*) I was poor.

ISOLDE (*claps her hands to her mouth*): Is it possible to be this poor!

SABINE (*with a gentle smile*): Much poorer, even. I was still among the privileged. I had bread.

ISOLDE: What do people do? They cry?

SABINE (*continuing to smile and with increasing self-confidence*): No. They work.

ISOLDE (*with a sideward glance at Sabine, the way one would look at an exotic animal, in a tactless tone of voice*): Aha.

SABINE (*inadvertently reacting to Isolde's tone of voice, she lifts her head and looks at Isolde with a beautiful, proud, and sad expression*)

RITTER (*clearing his throat*): Er—Isolde—loudmouth. Of course people work. Everybody works. I work too. (*Suddenly changing the subject.*) Do you play the piano?

SABINE: No.

RITTER: But you do sing?

SABINE: I used to—sometimes.

RITTER: Alto, naturally. Let's see. (*Goes to the piano.*)

ISOLDE (*to Carl*): You see how he is. A music maniac.

RITTER (*playing an octave*): Sing this line going up, la—

SABINE (*blushing deeply*): Oh please, please—I can't—I don't have a singing voice at all—I can't.

ISOLDE (*laying her hands on Sabine's shoulder*): Don't worry. I won't let him torture you. But Papa—leave poor Miss Graef in peace. Do you think everyone thinks of nothing but music, like you? Come here and be good, little Heinrich! (*Carl laughs, Sabine smiles.*)

RITTER (*returning to the table*): Let me see your hands. (*Takes Sabine's hands without further ado, bends them, and spreads the fingers.*) Very good piano hands. Very good. Strong yet elastic. And no long nails. Sensible, for once.

SABINE: Long nails are no good for surgery.

ISOLDE: Dreadful. Don't you faint?

SABINE: I've never fainted in my life.

ISOLDE: Not even when you see blood? I faint immediately. Did you perform surgery today?

SABINE: Several.

ISOLDE (*inadvertently moving away from her*): My God—there really is something cannibalistic about being a doctor.

RITTER: Didn't your knife slip just a bit?

SABINE (*smiling*): Slip—I don't think you've got the right idea about eye surgery.

RITTER: Well, then—did you do well today or didn't you?

SABINE (*embarrassed and faltering*): . . . Yes, I did.

ISOLDE: And you're not even telling us a hero's tale? You have to pound the drum a bit—

SABINE (*puzzled*): Pound the drum? What does that mean?

RITTER: Bonni—silly!

CARL: Viennese slang. Means to make much of oneself, to brag, shine a light on oneself.

SABINE (*shakes her head slightly*): A wretched gratification.

CARL: If one doesn't deserve it.

SABINE: Even if one does deserve it.

CARL: In which case, though, it would be understandable—for a genius—

SABINE (*timidly but with determination*): Isn't that—the weakness of kings?

ISOLDE: A king has more license than other people.

71

SABINE: It seems to me he ought to have less.

RITTER (*who has cleared his throat several times*): With your permission. The internal war among the sensual, the ethical, and the intellectual factors in the life of the common riffraff—

SABINE (*forgets herself for a moment, her eyes shining*): What about the royal riffraff?

ISOLDE (*interrupting*): Whatever, whatever— there have to be kings and princes and princesses. Isn't that right, Carl? The fairy tales are full of kings.

SABINE: And full of beggars.

ANNA (*has cleared the coffee cups and serves the mousse from a glass bowl*)

ISOLDE (*has risen from her chair and begun to braid Ritter's hair into thin braids*)

RITTER (*to Sabine, who helps herself to mousse*): Why don't you take a real helping? Stop eating like a bird, damn it!

ISOLDE: Charming invitation. Hold still, Chinaman. Else I will tear out whole tufts of your hair.

CARL (*shaking with laughter*): Chinaman, Chinaman!

RITTER (*to Sabine*): Don't you want a bit of fruit? (*Passes her the red currants.*) A few currants? Wagner liked them so much. Are you familiar with Wagner's works?

ISOLDE (*simultaneously to Carl*): Don't choke.

SABINE: Not at all.

RITTER (*incredulous*): Not—at all? Not even *Lohengrin*?

SABINE (*as embarrassed as at the beginning of the scene*): I have so little time—and if one has no talent—an interest grows out of a talent.

RITTER: Incredible! — How can anyone—

ISOLDE (*over his head*): Well, Papa, not everyone can be as clever as you. Such a smart cookie you are. Miss Graef, just look at him. He is Saint John the Baptist. John the Baptist fighting for the Wagnerian cause, that's what they called him, didn't they, Papa, when you were young?

RITTER (*half flattered, half smiling*): Yes—well, I helped beat down the doors a little to let the new art in.

ISOLDE: Back then, he was a revolutionary, the gentle little creature. But still, I don't have any respect for him. Are you my papa? Oh no, you're not my papa! You're my baby and I'll mollycoddle you. Look how thin he is. How the clothes hang down on him! God—how droll he is—such a poor little tramp.

SABINE (*in a low voice, touched to the core*): You love him very much.

ISOLDE (*kisses Ritter's hair*): One cannot help but love him. (*Pulls him up by a braid.*) Done! Now don't you go and undo it, my work of art. I don't see anyone eating, so I'll declare the repast concluded. Anyone who wants more can go back for more. Right, Carl?

RITTER: And now? A walk in the garden?

SABINE: There's still too much sunlight for Miss Isolde.

RITTER: How about a cigar, Carl? The ladies will excuse us for a few minutes. (*In a low voice to Carl.*) I'd like to take a look at the evening paper—I'm sure it's here already.

ISOLDE: Hm! Excuse you—ladies—

RITTER: You see, I can be diplomatic, as well.

ISOLDE (*has an idea*): Yes—Miss Graef, don't you smoke? Cigarettes?

SABINE: No, thank you.

CARL: Isn't that part of being a doctor?

SABINE: Not for me.

RITTER (*eagerly*): Right, right. Women shouldn't be like chimneys. Don't stay up talking, children, don't stay up talking. (*Goes off into his room with Carl.*)

ISOLDE (*calls after him*): Papa—don't put the lit end into your mouth. (*To Sabine.*) You know, he really doesn't know how to smoke, he makes a mess every time.

SABINE (*has sat down in one of the armchairs to the front right and looks at Isolde steadily*)

ISOLDE (*still standing*): Did I do something—because you're looking at me like that.

SABINE: No, no. I like you—like never before.

ISOLDE (*sits down*): Don't I know it—the dress is chic.

SABINE (*her head turned a little to the side*): How sweet you
were with him—how funny—and how much you
resemble him—at such moments.

ISOLDE: Resemble Papa? But Miss Graef—I am the spit-
ting image of my mama.

SABINE: I meant, how much you resemble him in character.

ANNA (*enters and clears the table*)

ISOLDE: Pardon me—Anna—leave the bowls, and the glass
plates. (*Turning again to Sabine.*) You were saying?

SABINE: You should always be like you are today.

ISOLDE (*leans back comfortably*): That's the way I am
around him—if I'm in a good mood. He really is
such a good little man.

SABINE: He is more than good. He is kind.

ISOLDE: And you shouldn't think that he's indelicate, because of his occasional coarse expressions. It's all in
good fun.

SABINE: But my dear Miss Isolde, do you regard me as so
indelicate as to think . . . He is as noble as children
are. Such a pure person. Such a young person.

ISOLDE: And he is still a poor little tramp. He always takes
everything so to heart. When I get worse—I only
worry about him. Then his face becomes so quiet—
so small and white—and there is something so soft
in his voice—oh, terrible!

75

SABINE: But isn't that your fault as well? You are not being truthful, Miss Isolde, you are not being truthful. You are keeping your father in a continuous state of illusion concerning your condition—and concerning the chances for recovery. I couldn't do it. I couldn't keep anything from him. I beg you—the next attack could affect him much worse—as it did on the first evening—I barely caught myself—and he still thinks that you still have half your vision in your left eye. You don't have a tenth, and you know it.

ISOLDE: I can't tell him. I'd rather be killed. Even if I turn as blind as a bat.

SABINE: You are wrong. Wrong. He is kind in his emotions, not weak.

ISOLDE: What do you know of him! I know him. It'll break him, really, it'll break him—my papa! You evil woman! (*Starts to cry.*)

SABINE (*jumps up in alarm and embraces Isolde from behind*): Dear Isolde—dear child—everything, just don't cry—just don't cry—you're harming yourself—please—don't cry.

ISOLDE (*quickly consoled, already with a half smile*): But if you torture me like this. You are the same type as my grandmama.

SABINE (*has sat down again*): And you, you are like all sick children. And a motherless child, at that.

ISOLDE (*with false sentimentality*): Aren't I? What I have had to bear already in my young life—so much misfortune. —— Do you like to attend balls?

SABINE: I've never been to a ball.

ISOLDE (*looks at her incredulously*): Oh!

SABINE: I cannot dance.

ISOLDE: You unfortunate woman. But how are you supposed to get married, then?

SABINE (*laughs heartily*): But I don't want to.

ISOLDE: Oh, everyone says that—if I hadn't fallen ill—I would have had a husband at nineteen—as soon as I was old enough to understand what marriage is all about. How old are you? I won't tell anyone.

SABINE: Of course—I am twenty-eight.

ISOLDE: Twenty-eight? But you have to hurry! Under thirty it's still just possible. But later, every man will think twice—an old maid.

SABINE: That's what I'll be.

ISOLDE (*looks at her inquiringly*): Have you set your heart on someone? An unhappy love story?

SABINE: Dear Miss Isolde—if you always have to work as much as I—you wouldn't even have time for an unhappy love story.

ISOLDE: I've been in love before—a hundred times. There are such interesting young men out there. Especially if they are a little bit arrogant. For a man, that is not a disadvantage, you know. Ah yes, men. The only entertaining thing in life. Carl is provokingly virtuous. Do you like him?

SABINE: I don't know him.

ISOLDE: A very nice boy, he is. But no taste in women. Well, one has to take what's available.

SABINE (*gets up, a little anxious*): I don't know, Miss Isolde— I don't understand you—but you make me so sad.

ISOLDE (*also gets up and takes Sabine's arm in a familiar manner*): You must confess to me. I'm sure you have had an eventful life and quite a few spicy escapades.

SABINE: Oh no!

ISOLDE: A lady doctor! But you can talk to me quite openly. I am anything but naïve. So, have you ever seen people naked?

SABINE: . . . Yes.

ISOLDE: Women—and men?

SABINE: . . . Yes.

ISOLDE: My God, that's really indecent. Do you enjoy it?

SABINE (*disentangles her arm and looks steadily in her eyes*): What do you mean by that?

ISOLDE (*boldly and innocently*): I suppose you must know a lot of things that other people, other girls, don't know. There are sometimes hints in books—but this must be quite a bit more explicit in medical books, am I right? Wouldn't a girl eventually get corrupted?

SABINE (*looks at her sideways*): It seems to me that depends on the person and not on the book.

ISOLDE: Did you always read them just to study? Or also because you were curious?

SABINE: Would you read such things because you're curious?

ISOLDE (*blushes, laughs, doesn't answer, and looks at the tips of her toes, moving her toes back and forth*)

SABINE (*presses her arms, which are crossed, closely together, as if withdrawing from Isolde*)

ISOLDE (*purses her lips and throws her head back*): After all, I am a grown woman. Secrets merely make people curious. You think about it—and it's pleasurable—on a sleepy summer evening—in the soft heat . . . (*She laughs to herself with her eyes half closed, turns her head back into her right arm, and passionately kisses her own left hand.*)

SABINE (*sorrowfully, only half to Isolde*): That on top of everything else! — Do you know, Miss Isolde, what I'm going to prescribe for you? A cold shower every day, and you'll have to get something to do, an occupation.

ISOLDE (*looking at her with great disappointment*): And that is all you have to tell me?

SABINE: Tell you? But what would you want me to tell you? In a sense it is possible that you know more than I do. And what I know wouldn't be good for such an unhealthy attitude—for this teenaged hysteria.

ISOLDE (*turning away with hostility*): Ah—you're like that.

SABINE: Yes, Miss Isolde, I'm like that. And you are too clever not to know yourself— ask yourself, honestly: could you look him in the eye—your papa?

ISOLDE (*has crossed her hands on her back, goes around singing*): *Schla Naninka doselli, doselli, doselli*— (*Speaking.*) Oh Lord, you didn't think I was in earnest?

SABINE: You were in earnest.

ISOLDE (*sings*): *Naterhalla lupeni*— (*Speaking.*) I love originality.

SABINE (*curtly and simply*): I don't.

ISOLDE (*gnaws her lips and tries to laugh*)

RITTER (*comes in with a newspaper in his hand, Carl behind him*): There you go again. Talk, talk, talk about everything, anything, but not a word about something that might actually interest you. (*Shows Sabine the newspaper, pointing to a section with his finger.*) You do know about this?

SABINE (*with a cursory glance at the section*): Yes.

RITTER: Then why didn't you say so at once? People like to enjoy such things with each other. (*Shakes her hand.*) Congratulations, congratulations!

ISOLDE (*to Carl, indicating Sabine with her head*): Is she engaged?

CARL: No, she got an award, from the Academy of Sciences in Paris. For an article!

ISOLDE: Money?

RITTER: Yes indeed! Three thousand francs!

ISOLDE: Surely now you will have a new dress made?

SABINE: First a few new instruments.

RITTER: Why don't you take a look how your name looks in print. Pretty good.

SABINE (*slightly uncomfortable, warding him off*): You think so? To me, there is something common about it, in a daily newspaper—it looks like an advertisement.

ISOLDE (*quietly, to Carl*): Doesn't she act modest!

CARL: And what wisdoms have you exchanged in the meantime?

ISOLDE (*with a meaningful glance*): Later. (*Takes his arm.*) I'd like to get some air now—in the garden.

RITTER: Still much too bright—much too bright.

ISOLDE (*pointing out with her hand*): It's twilight! (*Half singing, while she exits with Carl through the veranda.*) I will go flirt a bit—flirtate—

RITTER (*to Sabine*): Don't you think this will harm—

SABINE: Let her go. The exercise is good for her. She should get much more exercise anyway. We should change her entire way of life—her diet and—

RITTER (*alarmed, interrupts her*): Because of her eyes?

SABINE: No—not directly. Her eyes are as good as can be expected, given a chronic condition.

RITTER: I am so grateful to you. Oh, I'm telling you, what a relief to finally have a sensible doctor . . . because this improvement . . . that is your achievement.

SABINE: But not at all, Herr Ritter, not in the least! You are completely wrong. Any doctor could have treated your daughter in the same manner—

RITTER: Could have! But they couldn't! I'll go with success. Now she's got better . . .

SABINE: On her own, completely on her own. It's as much a mystery as the cause of the disease. (*Turning both hands into fists.*) That cause, that cause! It wakes me up at night—and there is no way of finding it out!

RITTER: Don't you start with that again! I still haven't forgiven you completely for that first evening. That was not nice, Miss Graef, that was not nice! Such ideas!

SABINE: You shouldn't judge me too harshly. I didn't know you then. As a conscientious physician I had to ask you the question that—hurt you so badly.

RITTER: Hurt me? It incensed me! And I tell you—

SABINE: You don't have to tell me anything anymore. The extensive observation of the disease has convinced me that my suspicion was erroneous, completely. Does that satisfy you?

RITTER (*looks at her, then exhales in relief*): Yes. I always felt somewhat constrained in your company.

SABINE: Sometimes it does leave you in the lurch—medical experience and rules—

RITTER: So much for all your famous modern science. Two times two makes four. Of course! As if there were nothing secret in the world! Mark my words, human beings shouldn't have too much brains. And you decidedly have too much brains.

SABINE: Do you think so? . . . I have an ardent request, Herr Ritter.

RITTER: Out with it!

SABINE: I would so very much like to hear you play.

RITTER: Miss Graef!! My fingers are like matchsticks. And I'm no longer in the mood for the piano. It's a dumb instrument. Orchestra and human voices, yes, that! And I am a piano player, not a virtuoso. I don't fit in with the present generation—at bottom, there was only ever one virtuoso—Liszt.

SABINE: Doesn't the past make him seem larger?

RITTER: Him? He played a glissando in such a way that you would have thought you heard someone laughing. And a chromatic wail of pain—not like the watery music of today. How naively he played Mozart—and in general—his prepotence of conception—and then his works!

SABINE: Have you never composed music?

RITTER (*looks at her and raises his eyebrows*): — — I don't have any ideas anymore. And you have to have an idea. It's not such a pity. Those few faked songs from way back then—I'm also lazy. If you don't have anyone with you who enjoys it—

SABINE: I would enjoy it so much.

RITTER: You? You antimusical being?

SABINE (*hesitates*): I did—as a child—as a very young girl—I learned to play a little violin. Oh, very badly. Just to accompany the schoolchildren singing—instead of my father—and because I was supposed to become a teacher, as well.

RITTER: And you gave it up?

SABINE: Completely.

RITTER: Sinful, simply sinful. I can tell just by looking at you that you would have been talented—

SABINE: I had to give it up because of my profession. The sensitivity of the fingers is blunted by pushing down the strings.

RITTER: Right, right—your silly profession. How did you end up doing this—something so unnatural?

SABINE: Unusual, isn't it?

RITTER: Female moodiness, I presume.

SABINE: No, Herr Ritter. My father suffered from eye disease his entire life and went blind shortly before his death.

RITTER: Was that long ago?

SABINE: Very long ago. Twelve years. And my mother—even longer.

RITTER: But there are still relatives?

SABINE: Nobody.

RITTER: You poor thing.

SABINE: It's better this way—I don't have any duties toward others—only a great duty toward myself.

RITTER: Duty, duty—such a purely utilitarian existence—it's just as if someone had studied all the tricks of counterpoint and couldn't find a melody.

SABINE: Yes, one exists as if in the shadow of a wall.

RITTER: Have you been away from home for a long time? Where is your home? In the north? Of course.

SABINE: Yes. At the North Sea. A small fishing village. I've been gone eleven years.

RITTER: Do you love it, the sea?

SABINE (*breathes in deeply*): The sea—oh!

RITTER: I'd certainly be seasick. Do you like that, such a big storm and the big breaking waves?

SABINE: That, too. But above all—the twilight. It lies there—silent in its gray holiness—you don't know its depth—but you can sense it.

RITTER (*looks at Sabine with a suddenly welling-up admiration; Sabine looks in front of her with her eyes open wide, breathing deeply, not moving. He bursts out*): Miss Graef, you are exquisitely beautiful.

SABINE (*blushes and covers her face with one hand*)

RITTER: It's all right if I tell you. You know, in a few weeks I'll be fifty—an old man—shaky—rusty—

SABINE (*half melancholy*): You are still young.

RITTER: Tell me more about you.

SABINE (*hastily*): No, no. It's no good: talking about oneself. One commits errors and then loses the feeling for one's own errors. Why don't you play a little for me—

RITTER (*shakes his head gently*): No, Miss Graef. For what? All of this is pretty much history anyway.

SABINE (*again raises her hands, pleadingly*)

RITTER: Don't take such trouble, Miss Graef. I am on the scrap heap now. You don't understand! — — You're young, that's why. When you're young, you like to push the pedal hard—forte—because so many stand around you and listen—later you're more alone, finally completely alone, and that's when you learn to play piano—pianissimo — — (*Takes one of her hands.*) By the way, you're a nice girl. Really a very nice girl.

SABINE (*stands before him, lowering her head slowly. He places his other hand on her head and looks down upon her, lost in thought*)

ISOLDE AND CARL (*come up slowly through the veranda*)

ISOLDE (*quietly and surprised to Carl*): Now look at those two! One might think that they had—

ACT III

The curtains are drawn closed.
A few rays of sunshine on the floor.

ISOLDE (*is lying on the sofa, pale, nervous, her feet pulled up*)

There is a knock.

ISOLDE (*from between clenched teeth*): Who is it now? (*Aloud.*) Come in.

CARL (*enters, dressed in a loden jacket, short trousers, and green hunter's cap. He is carrying a great bouquet of alpine roses in his hand*): Howdy, Bonni.

ISOLDE (*half with an effort, half cross*): Hi.

CARL (*puts his hat on the table*): Well??

ISOLDE: What?

CARL: How is it? With you?

ISOLDE (*with angry irony*): Ex-cel-lent. We haven't had the pleasure in a while.

CARL: Three days.

ISOLDE: Four.

CARL: And three hours, twenty minutes, and seven seconds. Surely, I'll be permitted to go out every once in a while. (*Hands her the bouquet.*) There.

ISOLDE: Bought?

CARL: What are you thinking! (*Pushes back his jacket sleeve and shows her a long scratch mark.*) I almost gave it up for this, my dear life.

ISOLDE: Yuck! You're wearing the hunter's shirt again— that always smells of sweat.

CARL: I can't climb the Zugspitze in a tux, claque, and patent leather shoes. Miss Contrary!

ISOLDE: You can leave any time.

CARL (*puts his hands in his pockets and marches about with great strides, placatingly*): Don't be a grouch—as they say out there. Is the farmer at home?

ISOLDE: Away—town.

CARL: Where? Why? What is he doing?

ISOLDE: Voice lessons.

CARL: He's giving voice lessons? To whom?

ISOLDE: To her.

CARL: To whom her? Can't you say more than three words in a row? Darn it!

ISOLDE: To the Graef woman. He had a piano brought into her hole under the roof.

CARL: She's learning to sing! Holy cow!

ISOLDE (*always from between clenched teeth*): Oh—she's got a beautiful voice.

CARL: Have you heard her?

ISOLDE: No. Papa says.

CARL: Well, in that case . . .

ISOLDE: And she's got individuality. And a lot of inner spirit. And independence. And meaning—and—God, I don't know what else.

CARL: That's what your papa says?

ISOLDE (*doesn't answer and chews on her handkerchief*)

CARL: Does she still stop by every day?

ISOLDE: No. Not anymore. The professor is back. He stops by twice a week, and sometimes she does, too. But he runs to her almost every day. Every—day.

CARL (*insecure*): And what do you think they—I mean—

ISOLDE: What they're doing—together? Nothing. Nothing at all. He talks to her.

CARL: She doesn't know anything about music.

ISOLDE: Her! Oh, she is a cunning one! Acting all not vain and not coquettish—but she wore new shoes recently—patent leather shoes with steel pearls at the tips.

CARL: I'm sure that didn't impress your papa. What can possibly result from these lessons? If a man likes a woman, that still doesn't mean it's anything serious. Come, you are working yourself up unnecessarily.

ISOLDE: Something serious? Even better! He's courting her. He's interested in her. The old ones are always the worst.

CARL: And in a few weeks, the grass and music will grow over it. Leave him be.

ISOLDE (*slowly, hesitatingly, finally dissolving into feverish tears*): And me? – And me!! I love him, and I am to play second fiddle to her, and have nothing—and all I have in the whole world is him, and I am so sick and miserable—

CARL: But do you think he loves you any less because of this? Don't cry, little hippo.

ISOLDE: He's supposed to love only me, only me. I want him all to myself—

CARL: But he does love only you!

ISOLDE: Yes? But he doesn't ask nearly as often how I am. He's distracted, and he plays so terribly much on the piano, and I think he's composing. And he's giving money for blind children.

CARL: If he's not giving it to blind children, he's probably giving it to Bohemian musicians.

ISOLDE: Recently I wanted to have a hat delivered from Paris—and he said no. No! He said no to me. It was too expensive, he said. Eighty francs, too expensive!

CARL: Eighty francs—you could buy an etching by Klinger for that!

ISOLDE: Before this, he wouldn't have refused me—it's all her fault, hers! Without her, he'd never ever have dared. (*Suddenly jumps up with a wild outcry.*) What do I care about the hat! But I want my papa back, my papa! Carl, if he doesn't love me anymore, if he loves her now, the clever one—then I'll jump out of the window, so they'll find me dead on the ground!

CARL (*dismayed, takes her in his arms*): Bonni, my dearest, only, sweet, golden Bonni—

ISOLDE (*trembling in his arms, pressing against his chest*): He doesn't like me anymore—because I'm sick and ugly and stupid and old—

CARL: But she's much older.

ISOLDE: But she's healthy! She is so cold and healthy! And I am sick and nobody loves me!

CARL (*passionately*): Bonni, there is one person, one—

ISOLDE: Yes, you—you are the only one who understands me—but you don't understand me either. (*Throws both arms around his neck.*) You—you!

CARL (*beside himself*): Isolde—the moment has come! Do you love me? Like Isolde loved Tristan—not just so-so—I mean, since we've known each other for a long time now . . .

ISOLDE (*pressed closely against him*): I have such a fear within me, such a fear—am I really still a little bit pretty?

CARL: You are beautiful, as beautiful as an angel—like a goddess!

ISOLDE: More beautiful than her? And do you like me?

CARL: My queen!

ISOLDE (*passing one hand over her hair*): Oh, I am so disheveled!

CARL (*holds her closely to his chest. After a few seconds he lets go of her, dismayed, and turns away from her, breathing heavily*)

ISOLDE (*disappointed*): Well?

CARL (*turns to her again*): Isolde—now you are mine. I will speak to your father. I will remonstrate with him. I could say that I have observed—

ISOLDE: But you have to do that very cunningly; I don't want him to know that I told you anything—he has to think that you yourself noticed—he can't get the idea that I'm jealous—I'm too proud to have him think that.

CARL: Leave it to me—I will approach this with all diplomatic composure imaginable—I am in the mood just now—

ISOLDE (*with a low lasting sound, taking her face into both hands*): Oh—oh!

CARL: Is something wrong?

ISOLDE: It's back—in the eye—there is such pressure—it feels like it's going to burst!

CARL: Again? Was it—during the past few days?

ISOLDE: Not during the day. During the past few nights. And then I lie there and swallow it down. Nobody asks me anymore anyway. I could die here—oh! (*Her voice fails, her face turning rigid with pain.*)

CARL (*runs back and forth aimlessly*): Do you want beer— water—or what should I—?

ISOLDE: No—to bed—please—take me.

CARL (*leads her into her bedroom and closes the door from within*)

The stage remains empty for a moment.

RITTER (*hastily pushes open the veranda door, sunlight flooding brightly into the room*)

SABINE (*follows somewhat more slowly. She is wearing a simple white dress with a black belt and a big light straw hat*)

RITTER (*continuing the conversation with ardor and anger*): And I'm telling you, our age cannot give up the right to feel as one with infinity. It must be the artist who— the artist must be a liberator of life. Art must be religion to him.

SABINE: And all the poor nonartists? The people?

RITTER: Artists and people can meet—there is one realm common to both—as I said, religion.

SABINE: Which religion?

RITTER: Christianity. Naturally.

SABINE: Which Christianity? Catholic, Protestant—

RITTER: I mean faith, the idea—

SABINE: Faith, ideas—those are floating coffins. There is no common ground for us here. You see human beings as the image of God. And I see them as the most highly developed animal form. I don't understand your divine truth.

RITTER: But it doesn't disprove my truth that you're too obtuse to understand it. Your animal truth is undignified, destructive.

SABINE: That doesn't disprove it, either. Only that which survives the hard school of rational activity—

RITTER: Rationality? What does it do? What can it do? A negative effect! The rational insanity of the French Revolution has shown us the consequence of rationality. What is it? At best? The gilded impotence of the soul.

SABINE (*smiling*): So do women have a soul? There was a medieval council that debated the question.

RITTER: You have one! No doubt about it. But it's in hiding. Out with it! Spirit! Silly happiness! I want to put you right back into the Middle Ages. Where there were still castles and knights and traveling bards—

SABINE: And neck irons.

RITTER (*is silent for a moment, then raging*): But you are the most insufferable woman I've ever met! (*Runs back and forth, grumbling.*)

SABINE: And you are so sweet—so sweet (*approaches him with her hands folded*). Scold me a little more, but don't be angry with me. What fault is it of mine that I'm suffering from intellectual scotoma? That I have such a limited field of vision? I know too many graveyard stories. And worse. Do you believe that all tragedies end in death? Please! Please!

RITTER (*still grumbling, but already somewhat mollified*): Well then—why don't you take off that contraption now.

SABINE: What—the hat?

RITTER: Yes. That contraption of a hat. I love to see the part in your hair.

SABINE (*takes off her hat*)

RITTER (*places both of his hands on her shoulders, forcing her to stand hunched slightly forward*): There—it's just like a fine line on a score. And now, let's not quarrel anymore. Now be a little nice to me.

SABINE: I really don't have time for this. I should first look in on Isolde—

RITTER: No time, again! No time to be nice. (*He pushes her down on a chair.*) Sit. There, you working woman. (*Pushes a chair up to her, sits down, his legs spread slightly, his arms resting on the armrests, his hands folded between his knees and moving up and down.*) Let me look at you. Not bad. Not bad. You're getting to be quite pretty. I like you. Do you know that?

SABINE (*does not answer, looks at him directly, her eyes large*)

RITTER: If you are very nice, I'll show you something.

SABINE (*brightening*): Something you composed?

RITTER (*laughs, with a contemptuous movement of his hand*): It's not worth a farthing. You'll like it. You don't understand anything. But you have to sing it.

SABINE: I? You know how afraid I always am of you. And you already gave me such a hard time today during the lesson.

RITTER: Because you never open your mouth (*sings a note with his lips closed in imitation of her*). Always with your teeth clenched. You will sing now. It does you good to read off the score. Your ear is good enough for three. Now! No silliness. (*He takes Sabine by the wrist and pulls her to the piano, where he rummages until he finds a crumpled sheet of music.*) Look at this— (*Shows it to her.*) B-major. Five sharps. Quite simple. (*Sits down and plays the root note for her.*)

SABINE (*accompanied by Ritter, sings, first shyly, then with increasing courage and spontaneous expression*):

> As pretty as a flower,
> Charming and pure thou art.
> I look at thee and sadness
> Comes creeping o'er my heart.
> I place my hands with blessing
> Upon thy head demure,
> Praying that God may keep thee
> So charming and so pure.

RITTER (*has looked at her angrily at "sadness" and yelled*): Open your mouth! (*They have finished.*)

SABINE (*looks at the floor silently*)

RITTER (*rises, utterly unmoved*): That was quite decent. Still too much dilettantish sentimentality. I have to change that tierce, by the way. (*Makes corrections in pencil on the score.*) I think that little romance has already been composed about 325 times. I am composer number 326. (*Since Sabine has remained silent.*) Don't you like it? Don't be shy!

SABINE (*quietly*): It is lovely.

RITTER (*sways his head*): Goodness, goodness! Seems to me I was thinking of you when I wrote it. Sometimes you've got something about you like the—what are they called—the dark flowers that open in the night—

CARL (*has opened the door to Isolde's room slightly, stood there a moment and now advances toward them. He is red in the face and insolently reticent*): My respects. (*Bows stiffly to Sabine.*)

RITTER (*still correcting his score*): Well, is it Carl? A good day to you! Had a safe return from the clouds? Nice view up there?

CARL: I would like to entreat you to postpone the musical recitals till another day. One can hear too clearly in the next room, and since Isolde seems to be very ill—

RITTER (*runs toward the bedroom door*): God in Heaven!

CARL (*holds him back*): Please—I do not believe that Isolde wishes to see you—after this concert.

SABINE (*steps between the two of them. Completely calm, she has adopted, once again, the behavior she displayed during her first appearance. She begins to speak during Carl's final three words*): Let me—I will see right away what it is.

CARL (*bitterly*): You could be wrong.

SABINE (*without reacting to his words*): Don't worry unnecessarily. It won't mean anything. (*Exits into Isolde's room.*)

RITTER (*falling into a chair*): — — Have you—have you been with the child long?

CARL (*still insolent, with stifled irritation*): A long time.

RITTER: I was with Miss Graef.

CARL: As usual.

RITTER: It's refreshing. I visit her frequently.

CARL: And Isolde is alone frequently.

RITTER: I would like to provide her with company—a few nice young girls—but if you don't know any family . . .

CARL: Exactly—to make her feel even more acutely the difference between her youth and that of other young girls.

RITTER: There, you're right. It's a dilemma. But what is a person to do? I do whatever is in my power.

CARL (*puffing himself up, with a withering glance and extended hand*): That, you do not!

RITTER (*turns around in his chair, incredulous whether he has heard right, half laughing*): Carl—have you lost your marbles?

CARL (*somewhat offended, but with the same pathos*): I intend to remind you of your paternal responsibilities . . . My manhood forbids me to continue to watch Isolde being further— mistreated.

RITTER (*wants to jump up, then reconsiders and says quietly*): Go on.

CARL: You are not mistreating her physically but mentally. Her smallest wishes are relentlessly denied. Nobody bothers about her suffering anymore. She is getting more helpless and lonely every day. Her youth and beauty are withering and dying—she is suffering martyrdom—you are nailing her to the cross— (*He bursts into tears, moved by his own words.*)

RITTER (*has got up and now walks up and down*): My dear boy, what you're blathering is blooming nonsense. Why don't you just cough it up now. I don't know who put this stuff into your head—well, why don't you just cough it all up first.

CARL (*deeply offended*): For you, this is a joking matter— unquestionably.

RITTER (*pauses in his pacing*): No, Carl—for me this is a tragic matter. (*With a gesture of annoyance toward himself.*) Damn it! Should I open my mouth about this—that I gave myself up—for my child? Of course one does everything for one's child—but I won't do a song and dance about it.

CARL: You couldn't, anyway.

RITTER: I wouldn't want to—damn it! I'd feel like a braggart.

CARL: But you are neglecting Isolde—compared with other people.

RITTER: Compared with whom am I neglecting her, compared with whom? I separated from my mother—because of her. Well and good, I understand that they don't get along, and I know quite well that most of it is Isolde's fault—but she is ill. So I left a seventy-year-old woman on her own.

CARL (*with childish malice*): Oh, how fervent you can become when you feel guilty. I was talking of a completely different woman—a young one.

RITTER: Let me tell you something, Carl. I don't have the patience for this, and I'm not in the mood—get lost. Tomorrow is another day. Maybe tomorrow we'll understand each other better.

CARL: Then there is only one more trifle.

RITTER: Out with it!

CARL: I have just had occasion to become convinced that you have relinquished not only your eternal but also your inner right to fatherhood with regard to Isolde.

You will be glad to rid yourself of her honorably. I will marry Isolde.

RITTER (*stands there with his mouth open*)

CARL: Isolde is twenty-one, that is, of age according to Austrian law.

RITTER (*coming out of his stupor and pouncing upon him*): And you are— (*Controlling himself.*) And you are not of age.

CARL: If you think you can dispose of me in this manner—

RITTER: And if you don't leave me alone with your grotesque ideas— (*Restrains himself forcibly.*) Oh well, well, well! You are young and extravagant.

CARL: You know very well that the early loss of my father and my own serious nature have matured me beyond my years.

RITTER (*already good-natured again, half laughing*): Proof: the young gentleman wishes to marry on a monthly income of—I can't figure it out to the last half-penny—just because you feel a bit of high-strung infatuation with a couple of blond braids—

CARL: I love Isolde as a man.

RITTER (*puts his hands into his pants pockets. Dryly*): Don't believe it.

CARL: I will prove it to—

RITTER (*interrupting*): Prove—I know, I know. And I will even tell you how you can prove it. You can prove it by leaving my poor girl alone with your foolishness. You haven't told her anything yet?

CARL: . . . No, but—

RITTER (*continues*): You can prove it by swallowing your unhappy love as quickly as possible. I cannot give her to you. Don't you see that for yourself? It would be an irresponsibility—also toward you.

CARL: Because you don't know the first thing about my heart, because you don't know what a deep, eternal feeling—

RITTER (*moodily*): Eternal feeling—stuff and nonsense.

CARL: I will take better care of Isolde than you, even if we'll be poor.

RITTER: You'll take care of her on pub grub?

CARL: Because I will love her more. You only love her on the side, as long as it doesn't affect your other interests. You don't know anything about sacrifice, about renunciation, you don't have any ideals—

RITTER: I certainly don't subscribe to yours. And now shove off. I have tried to persuade you in kindness and in anger. If nothing has got into that thick skull of yours, then you are either a fool or a cad. Do you want to have a duel now? I don't have any weapons here—

CARL (*retreating from him*): We are finished with each other.

RITTER: Fine, fine. For how long?

CARL: Forever. (*Goes toward the veranda.*)

RITTER: See you later. Day after tomorrow?

CARL (*walks off without saying good-bye*)

RITTER: And now he's offended, on top of it all!

SABINE (*comes out of the bedroom, her face pale and serious*)

RITTER (*moving to her*): Miss Sabine—I have just had a scene here—but how is it going?

SABINE (*evasively*): I will check again later—what went on here?

RITTER (*constantly stumbling over his words in his agitation*): That fellow—that Carl—I can't believe it—he wants to marry! Isolde! Him!!

SABINE (*smiling impulsively*): Oh.

RITTER: And his demeanor—such insolence—and how he lectured me—I don't love her enough—he loves her passionately—and eternally—and I don't have any ideals—because I don't believe in it, this eternity—

SABINE: Did he say anything to Isolde?

RITTER: No. Didn't. On top of everything else! — Finally, I couldn't help myself, I got harsh—not very—and now he's deathly offended and will never come again. That would be quite bad—quite! It's such a colossal exaggeration—but there's something touching about it.

SABINE: Are you saying you want to ask his forgiveness?

RITTER: What would be so bad about that . . . ? I'll ask for his word of honor not to speak to Isolde of this foolishness. Because what would Bonni do if he never came to visit again—the child has grown so accustomed to him. (*Suddenly remembering.*) But you haven't told me yet—you're so quiet— (*Crying out.*) Sabine!!

SABINE: Not so loud—above all, be quiet— (*She takes Ritter's hands, her eyes large and steady on him. He calms down under her gaze.*)

RITTER: Yes—yes— But you must tell me—

SABINE (*with some difficulty*): It is worse.

RITTER (*barely audible*): The left eye.

SABINE: . . . Both eyes.

RITTER (*releases her hands, repeating heavily*): Both—eyes.

SABINE (*quietly but quickly, in order to alleviate the anxiety*): Extreme increase of pressure on the left eye, which was present in a mild form the first evening I saw her. Pronounced glaucoma. No pressure on the right eye, but an iritis.

RITTER: But how, how!

SABINE: Her eyelids look as if she has been weeping, a lot. When you told me the story a moment ago, I thought— Has she been upset in other ways, emotionally? Extreme altercations sometimes lead to an increase in pressure—

RITTER: I don't know anything anymore.

SABINE: Her manner also seems changed to me—something hard and bitter—of course, that could be due to the pain.

RITTER (*turns his face to her and raises his hands, balled into fists, to his lips*): Help us—help us.

SABINE: There is help. Surgery.

RITTER (*sways. Sabine holds him. After a pause*): Is that necessary?

SABINE: It's necessary.

RITTER (*paces back and forth a few times to regain his composure, then stops in front of Sabine*): What kind of surgery?

SABINE: On the left eye. Superior iridectomy.

RITTER: Is it dangerous?

SABINE (*after a moment of thought*): It's not risk-free. The iris will have atrophied considerably.

RITTER: Not risk-free. — And when?

SABINE: As soon as the condition of the eye permits. Tomorrow—the day after.

RITTER (*always returning to one thought*): Not risk-free.

SABINE: Berger is a skilled surgeon.

RITTER (*whirls around*): Berger?! You!

SABINE (*is silent*)

RITTER (*repeating more urgently*): You! You!

SABINE: No.

RITTER: Miss Graef!! I trust you alone, only you— That is the only thing that makes it easier— And Berger won't object in the least—and even if he did—

SABINE (*quietly*): I can't.

RITTER: Why, what? You can't? Silliness! Why not?

SABINE: Because I'd be afraid.

RITTER (*half furious*): You'd be afraid? Womenfolk!

SABINE (*with humorous melancholy*): Indeed, I've learned to be afraid.

RITTER: Why are you afraid?

SABINE (*simply*): Because she is your child.

RITTER: But that's precisely why you must do me this one great favor—if you feel even a spark of love for me. — You see, I will ask forgiveness of your entire damn world of science. — I beg of you, I beg of you . . . (*unable to continue*).

SABINE (*struggling with herself*): But I could never again take a scalpel into my hands if this time—

RITTER: Well—?

SABINE (*shakes her head*)

RITTER (*exploding in bright fury*): You're a silly goose!

SABINE (*looks at him, suddenly overcome by deep wholehearted laughter*): Yes, Herr Ritter, you're right. I am a goose. And nevertheless you shall be proven wrong. I will conduct the surgery. And I promise you that the goose will generate the finest coloboma that ever—

RITTER (*half moved, half grumbling*): I don't understand that but I guess it's all right. Which hand will you use to cut?

SABINE: The right one—of course.

RITTER (*quickly takes her hand and kisses it*): Play well.

ACT IV

Gray rainy afternoon. The veranda door is closed. On the piano stool, a black jacket and Sabine's hat. On the sofa, crumpled pillows and a blanket that has half slipped off. On the table a bowl with roses in full bloom.

Ritter and Carl enter through the front door. Both wear hats and coats, their collars turned up, wet with rain. Anna behind them.

RITTER: No, just take off your things here. The hallway is so dark when it rains.

ANNA (*helps Carl take off his things and hangs his coat, turned inside out, on a chair, leaning his umbrella beside it. She carries Ritter's things into his room. As she is leaving, Ritter asks, pointing at Sabine's hat*)

RITTER: She is here?

ANNA: Miss is with Mademoiselle.

RITTER (*rubbing his red hands*): Oh, then you have to wait, Carl. Pure November cold. Something hot, a cup of tea, Carl?

CARL: No thanks.

RITTER: What a time! Well, my boy—all is well now. Do you want to sit here, or here? Or on the sofa? There are still the pillows on it—for Bonni.

CARL: When did she leave the bed for the first time?

RITTER: The day before yesterday. For one hour. We have to be very careful. Obviously! After such surgery. I stood at the door, I tell you, right at the door—I don't want to have to go through that a second time.

CARL: She was not chloroformed?

RITTER: No. Miss Graef did not favor that, and Bonni herself didn't want it. She took it like a heroine. Not one twitch, not one sound. Everyone was delighted. The assistant, the nurse, and the professor.

CARL: Berger was there?

RITTER: Yes. For those people, this is some sort of theater. He said, by the way, that Miss Graef had simply performed a masterpiece. He wants to write about it in the *Medical Weekly*. She generated the nicest coloboma that he had ever seen in his entire practice, he said. And the iris was so atrophied that it couldn't even be planted, and the sphincter—

CARL: You have become learned.

RITTER: What else have I heard these past three weeks!! And she behaved even more kindly! Didn't leave Bonni's bedside, applied every bandage herself, slept nights sitting in an armchair beside her—and so calm, so gentle—like a mother.

CARL: I'm sure it was flattering to her professional ambition—and perhaps there was also a certain calculation—

RITTER: Not a trace of ambition, I tell you. She really is such a rare creature, she cannot help being kind. She's not one of those whose convictions are on one side and their deeds on the other. There is a harmony between the two—

CARL: You are remarkably delighted with her.

RITTER: I have good reason. A capital fellow. All my respect. Such a strong sense of honesty—a real comfort in all this modern phoniness.

Pause.

CARL: Hasn't she asked—for me—at all?

RITTER: Yes she has—a few times, why you weren't visiting. Incidentally, I still have to have a few words with you before I let you in to see her.

CARL: You will not prevent me from the last—

RITTER: My dear boy, let's be perfectly clear about our mutual nice feelings. You think I am a tyrant, and I think you are a dear good child with a few screws loose. Yes. Yes yes yes. But because you're leaving tonight, for a long time, you shall see Isolde once more, in God's name. I really wouldn't know how to explain to her that you didn't come to say good-bye. Under one bloody condition. You will give me your word of honor that you won't speak to Isolde about—about—marriage and all that. Understood? How glad you will be in three years that I've been so cruel.

CARL: You are putting a stone upon my heart, for all eternity—

RITTER: Do I have your word?

CARL (*with pathos*): My word of honor as a man.

RITTER (*places his hands upon his shoulders*): God, Carl, I like you so much. And I am so grateful for every little happiness you have given to my child—

CARL: And your relentlessness—

RITTER: Because I love my child and you as well.

CARL: I swear to you—

RITTER (*interrupting*): Give your mama my best wishes, she shouldn't scrimp too much, and tell me if she needs anything. And to little Mimi, a kiss from Uncle Heinrich. Have fun on your holidays and study hard next semester. Where are you going?

CARL: To Berlin.

RITTER: Well then. Write once in a while.

CARL (*passionately*): Pages and pages—and you will let me hear how she is doing—the only one.

RITTER (*good-naturedly*): You shall hear everything. Every little cough.

CARL: Perhaps the hour will come when you will realize—

RITTER: Have the sausages when you're in Treuchtlingen, they're delicious—

CARL: I'll make a note of it. Oh, if you only knew how hard it is for me—

RITTER: For God's sake, don't get excited. If you do, I can't let you go in. Stay calm! I'm counting on you. I'm going to knock now. (*Knocks softly.*)

SABINE (*her voice from inside*): Come in.

RITTER (*pulls the door open a little*): Can we come in? Carl is here. He wants to say adieu.

SABINE (*steps into the doorway*): Please— (*Going into the room before him.*) Good day.

CARL (*bows*)

SABINE (*throws Ritter a quick questioning glance*)

RITTER (*answers with a reassuring motion of his hand*): Does Bonni's condition permit—

SABINE: Not to worry. (*To Carl.*) But please, do not permit her to speak loudly, or very much.

RITTER (*pushes Carl through the door*): There, Bonni— there is your loyal knight. But don't chat too long. (*He closes the door.*)

SABINE: Isn't that dangerous?

RITTER: He gave me his word of honor. And he is already in the transitional phase. He is dreadfully unhappy, and he'll have the sausages at Treuchtlingen. What did I want to—I wanted to ask you something. Right. Tell me honestly: is the eye disfigured?

SABINE: Not at all. The upper lid covers the cut in the iris completely. That is also why she is protected from excessive light.

RITTER: My mother already asked—of course, women-folk—vanity is always their primary concern.

SABINE: Of course you also prefer for this to have been done without disfigurement. And Isolde above all.

RITTER: After all, she's a young girl. Oh, I'm so happy, I tell you. Well, and you? Don't make such a wise face. It suits you so much better to look a little frightened, and dumb. Or beaming all over, like you looked when you came out of the surgery. Did you look funny in your white apron and white cap! Like a cook! What! In that moment I forgave you every-thing. All your godlessness and your materialism.

SABINE: But I believe in Saint Cecilia—

RITTER: But also without inner conviction—not uncondi-tionally.

SABINE: No, not unconditionally.

RITTER: You see—and that's why nothing good can come of it. Perhaps you'll lose it with time, that critical attitude.

SABINE: Then that must happen very quickly. I haven't told you about it all this time—matters with Berlin are getting serious—

RITTER: Serious—why?

SABINE: I have received further news today—I have prospects of going in four weeks, or even earlier—

RITTER: You want to leave us— And you think I'm going to let you?

SABINE (*blushes and straightens a little*): Oh—

RITTER: Well—could you even do that? How will you survive without us?

SABINE (*confused and moved*): No matter how—no matter how hard it is for me to leave you, it is my duty.

RITTER: Duty here, duty there! Now that you finally have a few people who are interested in you, you want to run away. You, go away! You can't go to Berlin! Nice hole! Every ass there is a smartass. What could you want more than what you've got here? The professor has the highest respect for you, all the assistants gush about you—

SABINE: I must work toward a completely independent position. And in a big city I can learn more and be of more use to others.

RITTER: Why do you need an independent position— so-called independent? You've got to be Doctor Sabine Graef! First of all, you won't make it, given the way of the world, and secondly, it doesn't count for anything. You will do your job regardless. Isn't that enough?

SABINE (*evasively*): But I've particular research projects in mind, and for that—

RITTER: Nonsense! Excuses! Miss Graef!! Are you really made exclusively out of science and humanitarianism? Isn't there any woman left in you? With your own feelings and your own longing?

SABINE (*wringing her hands sorrowfully*): There's no help for it. I must go to Berlin. I must.

RITTER: With whom will I fuss once you're gone? I haven't ever fussed as much with anyone as I have with you, except with Hanslick, that sinister Brahms devotee. There was such emptiness in me before you came.

SABINE: Because you're missing your profession, because you need activity—

RITTER: No. Even before that. With all the activity. Even with Elizabeth— (*He stops.*) Something was missing. (*Pacing back and forth, utterly lost in thought and quite inadvertently.*) I've always waited for something. And then you came, and I felt good, and now you want to go away again. I won't be such a fool. I won't let you. Period. That's it. You hear? (*At the last word he recollects, as if awakening from a dream.*) But wha— — but of course— (*Innocently.*) Now I finally got it. That's why! Don't you notice anything, dear? (*Runs to Sabine, who paled perceptibly at the moment he called her dear for the first time, and takes her in both arms.*) May I?

115

SABINE (*slowly sinks down against him, fainting*)

RITTER: Sabine—little girl—don't be so silly. I won't bite. Why don't you look at me!

SABINE (*slowly recovering*): Oh—excuse me—but— (*She motions at her heart.*)

RITTER (*putting her down in a chair*): Say something—otherwise I'll think you don't like me.

SABINE (*opening her eyes to him half sorrowfully, half blissfully*): If—if I am good enough for you—

RITTER: We'll see, little boy. We'll see. I'm quite content with you. You little baby face you! But the devil, I am too old for you. Finally I'll turn gray—

SABINE (*quietly but full of a nameless bliss*): Why don't you! I can take anything now.

RITTER: But I don't want to grow old. I want to stay young for my pretty beautiful wife—I want to please you.

SABINE (*from the depths of her heart, while pressing his hand to her chest*): Oh—you please me.

RITTER: Call me Heinrich, just once.

SABINE (*hesitates a little*)

RITTER: Well? Obey!

SABINE (*quietly and quickly*): Heinrich.

RITTER: That's the spirit. You will obey anyhow. No modern nonsense. That is: you can go on doctoring. (*Looking at her.*) Oh—do what you want. As long as you love me. No, I say, such happiness in my old age! I could howl with joy! And my mother! She will—be so— (*His voice breaks.*)

SABINE (*suddenly overcome by a shiver, indicating Isolde's door*): And—?

RITTER (*blissful, excited, mixed up*): Bonni? Well, if she doesn't—she should be kissing your feet! You saved more than her life, and you took care of her, on top of that, like half a dozen mothers! She'll be overjoyed! No, really, I know my child. Only we must be quick now. I can't wait to have you in the house. Tomorrow we'll say the banns—I guess I'll find my certificate of baptism somewhere—you are Catholic, right?

SABINE: No confession.

RITTER: Good Lord! Such insanity! You'll see what kind of trouble that will cause now! Didn't you think of me back when you did that?

SABINE: Six years ago?

RITTER (*exasperated*): No church wedding, then. Of course. Too bad! It would have been such a nice choir. But you'll wear a dress—I tell you that. A white one—bridal type. And a veil like that—pulled down over the head—and green leaves—you know what I mean. You will look good enough to eat. (*Places one arm around her waist and walks her around the room.*) Isn't this a thousand times better than the whole shabby medical travesty you've been playing?

SABINE (*her head at his shoulder*): Better—yes, it is.

RITTER: I will teach you to be happy. You will be spanked if you're not happy. And I will cure you of your cleverness.

SABINE: I want to become stupid—very happily stupid.

RITTER (*taking her head into his hands*): Look how I can touch you now. I can do that now, I can. This is my right. I can even— (*He pauses.*) Don't laugh at me. I don't have the courage to do that yet. There is something so beautifully innocent about you. Surely nobody has kissed you yet?

SABINE: Nobody—except for my father.

RITTER: Thank God. I would have been so unhappy if— But say something to me. Am I your ideal?

SABINE (*looks at him and throws herself into his arms*): Much better.

RITTER (*stroking her hair and rocking her back and forth in his arms*): My little alto voice that never opens her mouth when singing— (*Seeing that Sabine is weeping.*) But rascal, what is it—? Why are you crying?

SABINE: Because I'm so happy.

Pause.

SABINE (*extricating herself from his arms*): — Oh Heinrich—it must be late already. What time is it? I have to go home.

RITTER: Please—you are home.

118

SABINE (*rubbing her cheek at his shoulder*): I will be. But I have to go to the clinic—I have to check—this morning's surgery patients—

RITTER: Horn can do that just this once.

SABINE: No, I must apply the new bandage myself. Otherwise I won't have any peace. And today, when I— today it would be a sin! I beg you! Today I want to take all pain from the world. No. (*Hastily puts her hat on and pulls on her jacket.*)

RITTER (*grumbles a little as he goes into his room*): But I want to be the main figure.

SABINE (*again looks at Isolde's door, shaken by the same shiver as previously, then straightens proudly*): Even if!!

RITTER (*returns with his hat, umbrella, and top coat*): I will accompany you. In general, you will now become used to accompaniment. My bride is a lady, not a doctor. Your arm, please, Mademoiselle!

SABINE (*shyly offers him her arm*)

RITTER (*takes a few steps with her toward the veranda*): But you started on the left foot. Stop! Turn right! There! You have much to learn, my child. And now keep time: one, two—one, two— (*His count turns into rhythmic staccato singing: the melody of the bridal chorus from* Lohengrin.) Lalalala—lalalala— (*Exits with Sabine over the veranda. After a few moments, the door to Isolde's room opens.*)

119

CARL (*looks out, then speaks over his shoulder*): They took off—seems to me. (*Opens the door wider.*) Are you really allowed—

ISOLDE (*appears in the door. She is wearing a flowing white negligee, her braids hanging down but not tied with ribbons. Her face is pale and thin. Her eyeglasses are gray and considerably darker than the previous pair. She is alternately apathetic and excited, cramped and feverish in all her movements. Supported by Carl, she pushes herself forward with great effort*): I can't stand it in there any longer, everything smells of carbolic acid—and iodoform. I can't get the smell out of my nose. (*Sinks into a chair.*)

CARL: Why didn't you come out earlier?

ISOLDE: When she was here? I can't stand to see them together. When he runs after her with his eyes— Did you hear him singing a minute ago?

CARL (*sad and absentminded*): Yes, well—the *Gaudeamus*.

ISOLDE: He sings so much now—just like someone from the theater.

CARL: Well yes, because you're out of the woods.

ISOLDE: And because she did so well. Oh Carl, if only I had pushed my eye into the knife so that she cut my eye in two. I wish I had dared! I hate her, I hate her.

CARL: Bonni—she's off to Berlin, for sure, I heard them say it.

ISOLDE: Then he'll think of her. You'll see, he'll think of her. In the end, they'll write to each other. I don't want to. I don't want to be grateful to her.

CARL: But after all, if she saved you—

ISOLDE: She did what? How do you know I wouldn't have been in less pain if Berger had done the surgery? Oh—it is too horrible to lie there, and the blood— oh! She was like a piece of ice—she didn't tremble—

CARL: But she couldn't—

ISOLDE: I don't care if she took care of me a hundred times—she doesn't love me, despite all that. No love. She looks down on me—I can feel it. I won't allow her to despise me, I won't let her—oh, if I could do something to her, something so that Papa won't like her anymore—

CARL (*bursting out*): And I cannot save you! I have to leave you! Now! The only one who— (*He falls on his knees before her.*) And I'm not even allowed to tell you!

ISOLDE (*suspiciously*): What—are you not allowed to tell me?

CARL: Not even the weak consolation of pouring out my heart—

ISOLDE (*with a dry throat and raspy voice*): What—you know something—

CARL: I'm not allowed to tell you, I cannot break my oath—

ISOLDE: To whom have you—what have you sworn—

CARL: To your cruel father, that I won't tell you! Otherwise he wouldn't have let me see you again. And I'm going away. I have sworn upon my honor—

ISOLDE: That doesn't matter— you have to tell me—

CARL: Oh Isolde, I want to die for you—but I can't. I cannot live without honor—no student could. If you cannot guess it—

ISOLDE (*looks at him fixedly for a long time*): Guess—

CARL (*kisses her hands*): Your poor hands—hot as fire—console me, Bonni—I have to go away soon—my train leaves in an hour—

ISOLDE: Don't go—don't go away, Carl, don't leave me alone—

CARL: I have to go now—I've got my ticket for the sleeper car—

ISOLDE (*breaking into spasmodic laughter*): And so he goes away without telling me anything. (*Pushes him away.*) Go, why don't you, I know it all anyway!

CARL: You cannot know—the inconceivable.

ISOLDE: I am not as stupid as you think. It's as plain as the nose on your face! Why don't you go away, forever. The whole world is leaving me. Right, why don't you! You will all regret how you have become my undoing.

CARL: Oh Bonni, you devastate me. (*Looks at his watch.*) I must go! It is high time. Oh, permit me one thing. Oh please—one kiss. There is nothing to it.

ISOLDE: There's nothing to it at all, and you could have had one a long time ago if you hadn't been so stupid.

CARL (*embraces and passionately kisses her, tears himself away, grabs his umbrella, hat, and top coat and wants to run off across the veranda*): Farewell—forever. (*As he tears open the glass door, he is pelted by wind and rain. He starts back.*) Well—I guess I have to put on the coat after all—it's pouring— (*He opens his umbrella.*) Farewell Isolde—I am going into night. (*He leaves without firmly closing the door. It has grown very dark.*)

ISOLDE (*stammering to herself as if in a fever*): Stepmother— stepmother. (*There is a quiet knock.*)

ISOLDE (*doesn't answer*)

ANNA (*pokes her head in the doorway*): Mademoiselle alone— Herr Carl—

ISOLDE (*motions toward the glass door*): Is Papa—I want him—

ANNA: Herr Ritter long gone—with Fräulein Doctor at his arm.

ISOLDE (*twitching convulsively*): What did he—what did he do with her—

ANNA: Led her by arm.

ISOLDE (*writhes*)

ANNA (*coming closer, anxiously*): Papa will surely soon come—

ISOLDE: I don't need him anymore—I don't want him anymore. Bring me—bring me—why don't you bring me—

ANNA: Bring what—

ISOLDE: But I told you already—the red one—the lavender salt in the red box—because—I have a—headache—

ANNA (*goes into Isolde's bedroom*)

ISOLDE (*tears at the edge of her dress in silent fury until a few scraps hang down, tears the roses out of the bowl, tears the leaves off them and throws them on the ground, bites her hands until she sinks back, half conscious*)

ANNA (*returns, placing the red plush case beside Isolde*)

ISOLDE: Go away—I want to be all alone—nobody is permitted to enter—nobody.

ANNA (*slowly goes off to the front room*)

ISOLDE (*opens the top of the case, retrieves the flask with trembling hands, and tries to read the label in the twilight. With a deep breath*): That! (*In a very loud voice.*) I have the courage— I want to have the courage—and I want— (*She hastily undoes her braids, letting her hair fall over her shoulders. She stands up, shakes her hair back, and again reaches for the flask. Trembling with fever but in a loud voice.*) I have the courage—I really have the courage— Our Father—who—who art— Papa!! Don't let me die—I don't want to!— I have the courage— (*She tears the top off the flask, places it to her lips, and immediately throws it away from her, crying out and falling to the floor.*) I can't—I— (*The wind tears open the glass door, rain streams in. Isolde, shivering with the cold, emits one more groan and then lies unconscious.*)

RITTER (*comes hastily across the veranda, stamping his feet*): Lalalala—damn it, has someone again forgotten to close the door tightly— (*He tries to close the door against the storm. He succeeds, throws the bolt, and stumbles on. He has pulled a box of matches out of his pocket and tries to light one as he is moving forward. His foot strikes Isolde.*) Damn that footstool. (*The match lights, he looks at the floor, emits a piercing scream. The match falls and goes out.*)

RITTER (*dropping to his knees beside Isolde*): My child, my child—what's happened— (*He lifts her up, screaming loudly*): Anna, Anna—Baba—my child—Anna—

ANNA (*comes running in with a candle, Baba a few moments later*)

RITTER: What happened here—what have you done to my child—bring water—water—

BABA (*takes a glass from the serving table and throws water over Isolde's forehead*)

RITTER: Run—run! Into the city—get Sabine—my child, oh my child, don't die on me—get Sabine!

Anna and Baba run off.

ISOLDE (*groaning, with her last strength*): No—not her!

125

RITTER (*stands like a stone for a moment, sways, lets Isolde glide into the armchair, stumbles to the door*): Anna—the professor—get Professor Berger—himself—not Miss Graef—(*coming back into the room, half breaking down*). Not—her!

ACT V

Bright autumn day. The glass door is open. The wind has blown dry leaves to the doorstep. Cool sunshine in the garden. Ritter, hunched over, with a mournful, prematurely aged face, stands at the piano, tiredly staring into space. Isolde sits in the armchair, emaciated, with a translucent face and nearly white lips, completely blind. She holds a bowl in her lap with peas, lentils, beans, and rice and separates them carefully, feeling with her fingers, to place each kind into one of the four separate wooden bowls that are placed before her on the table.

ISOLDE (*turns her head to the door on the right, thinking Ritter is there*): Papa—take a look and see if this is right. I think I've put a pea in with the lentils—

RITTER (*approaching her*): I am over here, child, over here.

ISOLDE (*turns her head toward the sound of his voice*): Oh there, I thought you were at the door. (*Feeling the first bowl.*) Beans, all of them?

RITTER (*running his fingers through them*): All beans.

ISOLDE (*pointing at the second*): Peas?

127

RITTER: There is a lentil in there—two. Maybe you got the bowl wrong.

ISOLDE: I probably wasn't paying attention. And the lentils?

RITTER (*rummaging through the third bowl*): One pea. But it really does look exactly like a lentil.

ISOLDE: And the rice?

RITTER: That—that is completely correct. You're already a little master at this.

ISOLDE (*cheerfully*): Don't you think, I'm already doing much better! Remember the first time? I got everything mixed up. Now I'll soon get braiding work, and then I'll braid one of those pretty wastepaper baskets for you. Just as pretty as the most skillful blind people make at the Institute for the Blind.

RITTER (*pressing his fists on his mouth, as if to stifle a cry, and turning away*)

ISOLDE (*after waiting for an answer for a moment*): Won't that make you happy, Papa?

RITTER (*wearily*): Oh yes, my child.

ISOLDE (*puts the bowl from her lap back on the table, always feeling her way carefully*): I think I'll stop now. In the end, your fingertips always itch from all the feeling and feeling and you don't feel anything anymore. (*She rises.*)

RITTER (*makes an anxious movement toward her*): Be careful—you'll run into something.

ISOLDE: Oh you silly Papa, you don't know how good I am already at walking on my own. (*Puts out her hands defensively, but in the wrong direction.*) Let me try.

RITTER: You'll get hurt—

ISOLDE (*slowly walking toward her bedroom door*): Not at all. There—is the chair—and there—the table—and now I'll go around here—and now I'm walking directly to the door— (*Takes a few quicker steps forward and walks against the door.*) Oh!

RITTER (*approaching her*): You see—you see!

ISOLDE: It doesn't hurt at all. That was just an accident. I can't be distracted when I'm walking.

RITTER: I am so afraid—that you might fall—

ISOLDE: I won't fall, Papa—just go away—you'll see how nicely I'll get back to my chair again. Now I'll just have to learn—to walk for the second time. (*She sits down in the armchair.*) Here I am! Don't you admire me?

RITTER (*bending over her sorrowfully*): Yes . . .

Pause.

ISOLDE: You're very quiet, Papa—you talk so little—you have to go out more—out into town.

RITTER: There's nothing I have to do in town.

ISOLDE: So you can tell me stories. During the past six long weeks you haven't taken a step out of the house.

RITTER: There's nothing in town.

ISOLDE (*shaking her head*): But you must go again. You're so quiet.

RITTER (*takes her hand*): Let me just stay with you, Bonni.

ISOLDE (*caressing his hands*): Poor Papa. And you don't play anymore, either.

RITTER: If you want—should I play you some Chopin—the nocturne—with the beautiful second movement—

ISOLDE (*hastily*): No, no. You don't like to play it, anyway. And I don't like it all that much anymore . . . I will ask you for something else.

RITTER: Something else? What?

ISOLDE: I should have thought about it sooner and I always forget—in my carelessness. You know Frau Blättner's little girl, the one who reads to me—she really has a lot of talent for the piano—the little one—well—could you give her lessons?

RITTER: Have you heard her play, then?

ISOLDE: No—but her mother says she's very talented.

RITTER: Her mother!

ISOLDE: You could hear her once—and if it's true—give her lessons—for my sake.

RITTER: Whatever you want—anything, whatever you want.

ISOLDE (*quietly hums to herself*): "At the quiet hearth, in wintertime"— (*Stops.*) Has the mailman already been here?

RITTER: Yes, an hour ago.

ISOLDE: It's that late—was there any mail?

RITTER: From Carl—a few words.

ISOLDE: Really—what?

RITTER: He wants to know how you are—I'm supposed to report to him extensively—what should I write him? I don't know how to tell him.

ISOLDE: You can tell him calmly. Do you know what he'll do? He will cry terribly and throw himself to the ground and dig his nails into the floorboards—and when he's caught a splinter, he'll remove it with a disinfected needle. And then he'll compose a very long, tragic, exquisitely beautiful poem. That's it. So you don't have to worry about telling him.

RITTER: And Grandmama?

ISOLDE: Grandmama—perhaps it would be better if someone were to tell her—to her face.

RITTER: Tell her—who—me?

ISOLDE: Or me.

RITTER: But how? Should she come here?

ISOLDE: Couldn't I go there—go back—to Vienna?

RITTER: To—Vienna?

ISOLDE (*rubbing her knees, a little labored but gently*): I really don't know why I should remain here . . . after all, it's over. The professor himself said that nobody can help me anymore. And I'm really quite content.

I was thinking—there really is no longer a reason to be here. After all, we came here because of the professor. And if he can't help me anymore—

RITTER (*repeats in a monotone*): Can't help—anymore— But look, Bonni—you also didn't—get on all that well with Grandmama—

ISOLDE: Back then, back then. Because I didn't have to then. Today— I have to.

RITTER: Why do you have to?

ISOLDE (*gently moving her head side to side*): I have to, I have to. And things will be better now with Grandmama. Tell me, Papa—honestly now—have I become very ugly?

RITTER: No—certainly not.

ISOLDE: But my eyes—so blank and rigid—

RITTER (*in a low voice*): But nobody can see them—if you keep your glasses on.

ISOLDE: And I will never take them off before Grandmama. Never. You'll see, if I wear a fine black dress, one that's made in the Salon Spitzer—if I'm all slender and all pale and with the blond braids on the black dress—then people will still say: the poor pretty thing. And Grandmama will cry and love me a lot and practically burst with pity and pride. (*She laughs quietly.*) That's how it will be. Unquestionably. I know who I'm dealing with.

RITTER (*sorrowful and incredulous*): I don't know if you're right, Bonni—whether that can last—

ISOLDE (*hastily*): Oh yes, I'm right. I have become cleverer anyhow. Don't you agree, Papa? It's strange. In the past, I've always believed that I had to have this and that and that—and now I see that I don't have to have it and I won't be unhappy if I don't get it. If you've got your bit of food and beans and lentils and peas to play with—I really don't need anything else. (*Forcibly cheerful.*) Not even you, Papa.

RITTER: Don't say that, Bonni. It's my only consolation that I can be with you.

ISOLDE: That's very nice. But you can't stay with me forever.

RITTER: I want to stay with you forever.

ISOLDE: No, Papa, that would not be smart of me. You would soon be tired of me. Everyone always thinks initially that compassion will last forever. But that's simply not possible. One day, you'll be accustomed to the fact that I—that I—can't see and on that day, you'll be tired of me.

RITTER (*turns away from her with a gesture of despair*)

ISOLDE (*waiting for an answer*): Well?

RITTER: What?

ISOLDE: I thought you said something to me.

RITTER (*is silent*)

ISOLDE: You are monosyllabic today. You haven't even called me a goose. Are you sick, since you're not telling me off?

RITTER: No.

ISOLDE: Yes—no. No—yes. Papa. I will send you off to travel.

RITTER: Don't joke about this.

ISOLDE: I'd like to go a-journeying,

> Come back with tales to tell,
>
> So therefore I'll take hat and coat,
>
> Choose my direction well . . .

Therefore, Herr Globetrotter, you will take a journey.

RITTER (*beginning to guess her intention, with bated breath*): Where to? I have no business anywhere.

ISOLDE: Do you think the people who go traveling about are on business? You should take your mind off things—go to Dresden—Leipzig—perhaps Berlin.

RITTER (*observing Isolde closely*): No, Bonni.

ISOLDE (*stubbornly*): But why not? You've never been there. And now it's become the cultural center.

RITTER: And what will you do while I'm gone?

ISOLDE: Me? I'll think of you and I'll be alone. No. I mean, I'll be alone and think of you.

RITTER: Wouldn't you prefer me to be with you?

ISOLDE (*evasively*): Prefer? People prefer a whole lot of things, but if they don't get them, it's not a disaster, right?

RITTER (*quietly, beseeching*): Wouldn't you—want to come with me?

ISOLDE: Come with you? Where?

RITTER: To—Berlin?

ISOLDE (*jumping up, with all her previous fervor and excessiveness*): Never! Never! Never!

Pause.

ISOLDE (*sinks back into her armchair; she is trembling and digging her teeth into her lips*)

RITTER (*passes his hands over his forehead, goes to Isolde, and takes her head into his hands*): My child, my child— we will go back to Vienna. Both of us—but we won't live with Grandmama—not on that dusty Prater Street. We will find something out in the Cottage District—something pretty—with a garden. And there we will be together—and live—happily ever after.

ISOLDE: No, Papa, no, you shall not sacrifice yourself for me.

RITTER: I beg you—let me stay with you.

ISOLDE (*sits still, then emitting a tortured cry*): If I could only see you now, if I could only see you! – not for the sake of seeing, I just want to know what kind of face you have—the patient one with the calm eyes—oh, Papa, not the patient one, not that one! Oh, I wish I were dead, if I had only had the courage!

RITTER (*on his knees before her, kissing her hands*): And I beg you to live, to stay with me, with your old Papa, who has nothing left in the whole world but you.

ISOLDE (*tortured*): But I know, and even if you say no a hundred times, I can still feel . . .

RITTER: What do you know . . .

ISOLDE: About her . . .

RITTER (*rising and forcing himself to remain calm*): Have you still got that in your head—that foolish stuff? How did you get onto that?

ISOLDE: I don't have you anymore, anyhow. Even if you're with me. I don't have you anymore. So I'd rather give you up completely. I plan to become complete-ly reasonable. You like reasonable people better than unreasonable ones. I've already noticed that. So I want to become reasonable. To the extent possible.

RITTER: And I want to give you everything I can.

ISOLDE: Everything—except love . . .

RITTER (*quietly*): Love. Love.

ISOLDE (*reaching out to his face to caress it*): Oh Papa—if it were possible for you to forgive me—because it's my own fault that everything went so wrong . . . You'll see, I can still learn a lot of things. If you wanted to read to me sometimes from clever books— (*Somewhat shyly*): Kant—maybe?

RITTER: You good soul. No, no. Can't strain your poor head.

ISOLDE: But it isn't all that poor anymore. I'm not in pain anymore. That's a great relief already. Oh, that pain—toward the end—when the vision went—

RITTER: Don't think of it, Bonni. Think of Vienna—and how we should furnish the apartment there.

ISOLDE: Papa! Surely there'll be poor children in Vienna as well. Don't you think I could start a school for small children—think about it—and give them all new aprons—and if there are many clever ones among them—perhaps there'll be one among them with a genius that would otherwise be lost—wouldn't that be noble of me—of us—because you must help too—

RITTER: To build castles in the air.

ISOLDE: I've got this mountain of time—

ANNA (*comes up hastily across the veranda and hands a card to Ritter*)

RITTER (*pales and blushes alternately, puts his finger to his lips and asks, hardly audible*): Where?

ANNA (*points out to the garden*)

RITTER: Please.

ANNA (*goes off into the garden*)

ISOLDE: Papa—is someone here?

RITTER: It was Anna—she'll be right back. Don't you want to go out into the garden with her? Before the sun goes down? Afterward it'll be too wet. You've spent so little time outside today.

ISOLDE (rises): Yes—but she's not allowed to lead me.

RITTER (*calls out into the garden*): Anna!

ISOLDE: She is to walk next to me. I will walk on my own and count my steps—

RITTER: Just be careful.

ISOLDE: I already know exactly how many—even around the rotunda—I've got twelve steps from here to the door. (*Counts as she walks.*) One, two, three, four, five, six, seven, eight, nine, ten, eleven, twelve— (*Stops.*)

RITTER: Two more, child, two more.

ISOLDE (*annoyed*): Oh—I must have made the steps too short—how stupid!

ANNA (*has come up the stairs again, accompanied by Sabine, who stops and presses herself as tightly as possible against the door frame of the side door*)

ISOLDE: So where is Anna?

ANNA (*steps to her side and takes her arm*)

ISOLDE: You can lead me down the steps, but then let go of me at once. (*Slowly descends the steps with Anna.*)

SABINE (*enters. Black dress. Very pale, with dark rings under her eyes*)

RITTER (*takes a few steps toward her. They stand in the middle of the room, facing each other silently*)

SABINE (*looks at his hunched-over figure with acute sorrow*)

RITTER (*finally, a gesture at the garden*): Blind.

SABINE (*in a low voice*): I know.

Pause.

SABINE: I wouldn't have come against your wishes—if I hadn't—

RITTER: Please sit down.

SABINE (*goes to the other side of the room, sits down in Isolde's chair, takes her hat off*)

RITTER: Did you—I wrote to you—didn't I write to you?

SABINE: Yes.

RITTER: Were you able to understand my letter? I'm sure it was incomprehensible— I was so beside myself—

SABINE: I understood everything. Isolde wanted to take her own life because we—

RITTER: Because the two of us—and she went blind. And the fever—oh!! Snuffed out—every ray of light.

SABINE: Glaucoma in both eyes. I know—Berger told me.

RITTER: Please forgive me—but I couldn't permit you to come here anymore. She would have lost her mind. And I couldn't leave her either. I know there was gossip. That you had botched the surgery—that the treatment was wrong—

SABINE: Oh, that! Let people talk. I only thought of you.

139

RITTER: We told Isolde that you had gone to Berlin suddenly—to start your new position—

SABINE: That's why I came. I'm supposed to leave tomorrow.

RITTER (*cut to the core*): Tomorrow!

SABINE (*rises*): Should I? – Heinrich?

RITTER (*with his hands over his eyes*): Yes.

Pause.

RITTER: I cannot abandon her—she's blind—and so I must abandon you.

SABINE: You don't have to. I have finally thought it all out, during these many nights. I will give up my job. Everything. I will go with you and take care of her. I will want nothing for myself. I will be so economical. I will do everything she asks. Just let me be with you. Just let me be with you.

RITTER: You precious creature—even if I could really accept your life as a gift—it wouldn't work. That least of all. She would pine and pine away—now I know.

SABINE: But what do I want? I want nothing from you! Understand me, Heinrich. Nothing. Not your name, not—you! Take me into your house as a nurse—for her. Only let me be here. Only don't be alone. So alone—so absolutely alone—God in Heaven, even if she was your wife, she couldn't refuse me this!

140

RITTER: She wouldn't refuse you—maybe not—but she would fret herself to death. Try to talk reason! Try to talk reason to a blind creature. Try asking a blind person for that selflessness when we healthy people cannot offer it. She's right, after all. She's right a thousand times over. I don't love her—as much as I love you. And you love me. She would be superfluous between us. Well, naturally! When all is said and done— (*He pushes the tips of his fingers into the corners of his closed eyelids.*)

SABINE (*stares down in front of her*)

RITTER: Sabine, I know very well that you are telling yourself that I'm a weakling. I also know what would be the stronger thing to do. To embark with you into a new, active life—come what may—and may the devil take everybody else—

SABINE: Then come! Then come!

RITTER: I wish I could! I am simply too weak. I don't have a bit of talent to play a hero. I'm a poor fool, and I'm crawling into my corner.

SABINE: Is she really worth it, your suffering that much for her?

RITTER: I don't know. All I know is that she is blind. Blind because of us.

SABINE (*makes a gesture*)

RITTER: Don't! You won't persuade me otherwise. Oh!! I've taken on a whole bag full of sins. How can I

look you in the eye! And what have I done to you!—
Can't you forget me quickly?

SABINE (*smiling sorrowfully*): Don't think so.

RITTER: Erase me. Just remember how badly I've behaved toward you. Oh God! Forgive the old fool
that he liked you too much. (*He strokes her hair, murmuring lovingly. Catching himself.*) Yes—well. — How
bad I am at saying good-bye. I am so common.

SABINE (*bursting out*): But I'm dying, I'm dying—

RITTER (*grasping her hands, with deep, innermost feeling*):
Not you! You have what it takes to transcend your
sorrow. You could become one of those human beings who can see beyond all others—quiet and mag-
nificent. They usually don't know it themselves. But
the old man above will notice.

SABINE (*stands before him, trembling, her face aglow, beside
herself*): But I am not what you think—what you
think I am because you are that way—I am not
good—not calm—if I could have been with you, I
would have got over it—but to go away forever, forever, and never— (*She presses her hands into her chest.*)
There! There! (*She falls on her knees before him.*)

RITTER (*forgets everything and pulls her up to him*): My
wife—my wife! (*As he is trying to kiss her lips, he looks
at her face and is captured by her eyes*). My wife . . . I
cannot do this to you. Not this. (*Remains immobile,*

*lost completely in her eyes for a few seconds, then releases
her hands and folds his own in front of his lips.)* Pray-
ing—that God may—I'm a despicable old fellow. Perhaps you'll say—I'm a coward. But how can I do this
to you! To you! Don't despise me. Don't despise me!

SABINE *(crying out)*: Heinrich! You saintly man— *(Looks
up at him, her head sideways, her hands clasped like a
child.)* Now I have peace. Now I'll go. *(She turns
away from him and walks slowly. He tries to follow her;
she turns him away, her hand extended backward.)* I
cannot see you again. If I see you—then I can't go.
(She disappears down the stairs into the garden.)

RITTER *(looks after her for a long time, then sits down at the
piano and weeps bitterly)*

Twilight falls.

ISOLDE *(her voice from the garden)*: No, I want to carry it, I
want to give it to him myself, he'll be so pleased!

RITTER *(straightens, dries his eyes, and blows his nose violently)*

ISOLDE *(stumbling hastily up the stairs, a bushel of badly dismantled late roses in her hand, Anna behind her)*: Papa,
today is the fourteenth. Your birthday! And now I have
nothing but these last roses! But I plucked them myself. And just think, I can tell by scent whether they're
red or white. There—but where are you, Papa?

RITTER *(has risen and walked up to her)*: Here, my child.

ISOLDE: Aren't they beautiful? How do they look?

143

RITTER: Very beautiful. Don't get pricked—there are many thorns.

ISOLDE: Anna should put them into the Venetian vase.

RITTER (*gives Anna the roses*): Right.

ANNA (*exits to the front room*)

ISOLDE (*searching for Ritter with her arm*): And now give me a kiss, dear Papa. That cheered me right up. (*He kisses her.*) Is your cheek wet?

RITTER (*wipes it with his handkerchief*): No—I don't know.

ISOLDE: You turned fifty today, didn't you? I wouldn't want to get any older than that. And then you'll be eighty. I'm telling you now, Papa. When you die, I'll kill myself as well. And that time, I'll have the courage.

It grows darker and darker.

ISOLDE: It's made me tired—the walk in the garden. It must be getting on toward evening?

RITTER: Yes. It's late.

ISOLDE: Is the sun still up?

RITTER: No. The sun is gone.

ISOLDE: Come to me, Papa. It's dark, then. As a child, I was afraid in the dark, but now I'm not afraid anymore. Because I'm always in the dark. Will there be a moon tonight?

RITTER: A full moon. Over there—it's rising above the trees now—look (*remembering*). Right, well.

ISOLDE: Papa, when you tell me about it, I can see it before my inner eye. I'm not blind at all, I can see from the inside. Splendid visions. Only everything is black. It's not that bad at all . . . One can also live in the dark.

RITTER *(has drawn her to his chest)*: Yes, my child—one can also live in the dark. *(They stand there in a tight embrace. Bright moonlight shines on them.)*

The End

Modern Language Association of America
Texts and Translations

Texts

Anna Banti. *"La signorina" e altri racconti.* Ed. and introd. Carol Lazzaro-Weis. 2001.

Adolphe Belot. *Mademoiselle Giraud, ma femme.* Ed and introd. Christopher Rivers. 2002.

Dovid Bergelson. *Opgang.* Ed. and introd. Joseph Sherman. 1999.

Elsa Bernstein. *Dämmerung: Schauspiel in fünf Akten.* Ed. and introd. Susanne Kord. 2003.

Isabelle de Charrière. *Lettres de Mistriss Henley publiées par son amie.* Ed. Joan Hinde Stewart and Philip Stewart. 1993.

Sophie Cottin. *Claire d'Albe.* Ed. and introd. Margaret Cohen. 2002.

Claire de Duras. *Ourika.* Ed. Joan DeJean. Introd. Joan DeJean and Margaret Waller. 1994.

Françoise de Graffigny. *Lettres d'une Péruvienne.* Introd. Joan DeJean and Nancy K. Miller. 1993.

M. A. R. Habib, ed. and introd. *An Anthology of Modern Urdu Poetry.* 2003.

Sofya Kovalevskaya. *Nigilistka.* Ed. and introd. Natasha Kolchevska. 2001.

Thérèse Kuoh-Moukoury. *Rencontres essentielles.* Introd. Cheryl Toman. 2002.

Emilia Pardo Bazán. *"El encaje roto" y otros cuentos.* Ed. and introd. Joyce Tolliver. 1996.

Marie Riccoboni. *Histoire d'Ernestine.* Ed. Joan Hinde Stewart and Philip Stewart. 1998.

Eleonore Thon. *Adelheit von Rastenberg.* Ed. and introd. Karin A. Wurst. 1996.

Translations

Anna Banti. *"The Signorina" and Other Stories.* Trans. Martha King and Carol Lazzaro-Weis. 2001.

Adolphe Belot. *Mademoiselle Giraud, My Wife.* Trans. Christopher Rivers. 2002.

Dovid Bergelson. *Descent.* Trans. Joseph Sherman. 1999.

Elsa Bernstein. *Twilight: A Drama in Five Acts*. Trans. Susanne Kord. 2003.

Isabelle de Charrière. *Letters of Mistress Henley Published by Her Friend*. Trans. Philip Stewart and Jean Vaché. 1993.

Sophie Cottin. *Claire d'Albe*. Trans. Margaret Cohen. 2002.

Claire de Duras. *Ourika*. Trans. John Fowles. 1994.

Françoise de Graffigny. *Letters from a Peruvian Woman*. Trans. David Kornacker. 1993.

M. A. R. Habib, trans. *An Anthology of Modern Urdu Poetry*. 2003.

Sofya Kovalevskaya. *Nihilist Girl*. Trans. Natasha Kolchevska with Mary Zirin. 2001.

Thérèse Kuoh-Moukoury. *Essential Encounters*. Trans. Cheryl Toman. 2002.

Emilia Pardo Bazán. *"Torn Lace" and Other Stories*. Trans. María Cristina Urruela. 1996.

Marie Riccoboni. *The Story of Ernestine*. Trans. Joan Hinde Stewart and Philip Stewart. 1998.

Eleonore Thon. *Adelheit von Rastenberg*. Trans. George F. Peters. 1996.